END TIMES WARFARE PRAYER

PRAYERS TO BREAK THE POWERS OF THE DEVIL

ELOU FLEURINE

Copyright © 2020 by Elou Fleurine (MBA)

All rights reserved. No part of this publication may be reproduced, distributed, or transmitted in any form or by any means, including photocopying, recording, or other electronic or mechanical methods, without the prior written permission of the author, except in the case of brief quotations embodied in critical reviews and certain other noncommercial uses permitted by copyright law. Permission will be granted upon request.

All Scriptures quotations in the book are from the King James Version of the Bible. All Greek and Hebrew from the strong Bible Dictionary.

END TIMES WARFARE PRAYER

For information contact:
1001 NE 15 ST
Homestead, FL 33030
http://www.kingjesush.org

Book and Cover design by Digital Publishing of Florida
ISBN: 978-1-949720-58-7

First Edition: July 2020

CONTENTS

INTRODUCTION 5

1. Why We Need To Pray 7
2. Spiritual Battle 10
3. The Nature Of The Battle 14
4. War Prayer 20
5. Techniques To Conduct A Spiritual Warfare 25
6. Prayer Of Intercession And Spiritual Warfare 36
7. Prayer Against Death 45
8. Declarations And Prayers 53
9. Categories Of Prayer 69
10. Prayer Against Generational Curses 80
11. Prayer Against Jezebel Spirit Manipulation And Control 95

12. Divine Healing Prayer For All Type Of Sickness 101

13. Prayer For Finances 109

14. Prayer For Marriage That Is Going Through Problems 130

15. Prayer Of Overcoming The Flesh 136

ABOUT THE AUTHOR 151

ACKNOWLEDGMENTS 152

INTRODUCTION

Prayer is one of the essential Christian activities. Through prayer, a person maintains an intimate walk with the Lord and lays the foundation for other spiritual activities' success. Prayer also guarantees victory in the fight against Satan, as we commit ourselves by faith to protect and care for the Great Victor Jesus Christ. Dr. Myles Munroe said: "Prayer is like giving authorization to God to act on our behalf". One day the disciples' request to Jesus about this tool: "Lord, teach us to pray" (Luke 11: 1). We can only learn the art of sincere prayer and intercession from the Great Intercessor Jesus Christ. It is a school in which we must grow in grace and knowledge (2 Peter 3:18). Although prayer, in its original form, is so simple that even the smallest child can pray, at the same time, it is the highest form of dedication to which believers are called.

Jesus' disciples need to know how to pray. In a chaotic and troubled world like ours, prayer is a weapon of war to transform the reality around. We do not intend to do an elaborate theology of prayer, but to deal with this topic simply and punctually, in such a way that you feel encouraged to speak with God much more often, and that your moments of prayer are more pleasant.

You are about to start an exciting spiritual adventure. Through the pages of this book, you will learn about a powerful supernatural resource available to the body of Christ, intercessory prayer. In this study, you will learn how to fight the devil, what intercessory prayer is, and how to do it effectively using the dynamic spiritual resources that have been delegated for this purpose. You will learn what to pray for, how to overcome the hindrances to intercessory prayer, and how to start and stay. Your spiritual life and ministry will never be the same again.

This book is based on personal experience over the years, the battles I have conducted against the devil and his cohort of wicked agents. Whether you're a long-time prayer warrior or a novice, you'll find prayers to grow your communication with God as you seek His will in your life and those of others.

This book is not written only for believers but for everyone. It can be used as a resource for praying and teaching. This book will help you communicate with God with confidence, power, grace, and mercy.

1

WHY WE NEED TO PRAY

Prayer is not merely talking to God, but it also involves listening to Him. It is a religious act in which man seeks to maintain a connection with God through supplication, thanksgiving, praise, worship, among other purposes. Sometimes through prayer God will provide you with a special message of encouragement to share with someone you are interceding. Prayer is the dialogue of the believer towards God. This means that praying is talking to God. If God speaks to us through scripture, we talk to Him through prayer. So, prayer is a fundamental part of our relationship with the Lord. Through prayer, based on Christ's merits, we can have a life of communion with God. The true Christian understands that prayer must be a constant practice throughout his life. Prayer is one of the most mysterious aspects of the Christian walk. We wonder if God hears our prayers if our prayers influence our lives, about what it is acceptable to pray about, how we should pray, and so on. So why do we do it? Many reasons. We pray because it is a privilege. Prayer is your invitation to meet God. It allows us to come closer to Him. In fact, Prayer is our way of communicating with God. Just as friends and family members talk to each other to deepen their relationships, prayer deepens our relationship with God.

THE NEED OF PRAYER

Throughout the Bible, we see examples of people crying out and being attended to. Prayer is essential and plays some vital roles in our life with God. We must always know we build a relationship with quality time and suitable conversations. Therefore, praying to God brings you closer to understanding who He is and how He understands. This makes us understand His ways and purposes and feeds our spirit.

PRAYER IS MANDATORY

The first thing you must know about prayer is that you cannot live without it. Prayer is for the soul, just as food is for the body. In the same way that your body, if not fed, will get sick, so is your soul if not cared for. In Ephesians 6:18, we read: "Praying at all times with all prayer and supplication in the Spirit". Praying all the time may seem difficult if you accept prayer only as a moment kneeling before God, but it can be easy if you consider it as a conversation with God that you will have throughout the day. You can start your day with a few minutes of prayer, and during the day, in the intervals between works, in traffic, or in the face of every tough situation that presents itself, make brief prayers to God.

The temptations we are daily exposed make prayer a necessity. For God's power to guard us through faith, the desires of the mind must continually rise in silent prayer, pleading for help, light, strength, and knowledge. But reflection and prayer cannot take the place of intense and faithful use of time. It requires prayer and works to improve the Christian character.

PRAY FOR OTHERS

You can pray for relatives, for your pastor, for the members of your church, for the needy, for salvation in your city, for an end to corruption, or even create a list of these requests to remember none. Pray with faith and remember that "prayer made by a righteous person can have a lot of effects" (James 5:16). Remember that we, though found to be unjust in ourselves, to consider righteous because of Christ. We must pray to strengthen our relationship with God; it is always also important to pray for others. Whether to free captives spiritually, to heal or enhance a brother, or to rebuke Satan Prayer is a necessity.

2

SPIRITUAL BATTLE

The term "battle" refers to a struggle from someone against another, and the term "spiritual" refers to something that belongs to the spirit, which it does not connect the body to. For us, Christians, the spiritual battle is a battle that aims to keep us from God. Apostle Paul, in his letter to the Ephesians, already warns us: *"For it is not against men of flesh and blood that we have to fight, but against the principalities and powers, against the princes of this dark world, against the spiritual forces of evil (scattered) in the air"* (Eph 6, 12). So, who should we fight against?

The spiritual battle is a fight against us, against the world and the devil. Against ourselves, it refers to the battle against our lust, against our weaknesses, such as laziness, envy, greed, against the world, which today spills on us a flood of anti-Christian ideals, such as the culture of death, the incessant search for power, for possessing and for pleasure. At first, these ideas enter our daily lives and, now, try to steal our families, our principles, our morals.

There are two basic mistakes when talking about spiritual warfare: overemphasizing and underestimating it. Some blame every sin, every conflict, and every problem on demons that need to be cast out. Others ignore spiritual reality, and that the Bible teaches us that our battles are against spiritual powers. The key to success in spiritual warfare is finding a biblical balance. Sometimes Jesus cast out demons from the people, and sometimes he healed the people without mentioning the demonic.

The apostle Paul taught Christians to fight battles against sin in themselves (Romans 6), and to fight battles against the evil one (Ephesians 6: 10-18). Ephesians 6: 10-12 declares, "Behold, my brethren, be strong in the Lord, and in the power of his strength. Put on all the armor of God, so you can stand firm against the snares of the devil".

Because we do not have a fight against blood and flesh, but against principalities, against powers, against the rulers of darkness of this century, against spiritual hosts of evil in the celestial regions. This passage teaches us some crucial truths:

1) We can only be strong in the power of the Lord.

2) It is the armor of God that protects us.
3) Our battle is against the spiritual forces of evil in the world.

Ephesians 6: 13-18 gives us a description of the spiritual armor that God gives us. We must stand firm with:

(a) The belt of truth,

(b) The breastplate of justice,

(c) The gospel of peace,

(d) The shield of faith,

(e) The helmet of salvation,

(f) The sword of the spirit.

What do these pieces of spiritual armor represent to us in spiritual warfare?

They represent the truth to believe and to declare it. We must rest on the fact that we claim righteousness by the sacrifice that Christ made for us. We must proclaim the gospel, no matter how much resistance we receive. We should not hesitate in our faith, trusting in God's promises no matter how hard they attack us. Our maximum defense is the security we have of our salvation, a guarantee that no spiritual force can take away. Our offensive weapon is the Word of God, not our own opinions and feelings. We must pray in the power and will of the Holy Spirit.

These were Jesus' words to his disciples on one occasion when He taught them about prayer. Every disciple of Jesus must have a desire to learn to pray, and more than that, they must learn to use prayer as a powerful tool for every situation. In the war of conquest in which we insert, we do not fight against people (Eph. 6.12), so our weapons are not physical, but spiritual (II Co 10.3.4). Prayer is the most powerful spiritual weapon that God has left us. A word of caution concerning spiritual warfare would be appropriate. The name of Jesus is not a magical incantation that makes demons flee from before us. The seven sons of Sceva are an example of what can happen when people boast of an authority that has not been given to them (Acts 19:13 - 16). Even Archangel Michael did not rebuke Satan in his power, but said, *"The Lord rebuke you!"* (Jude 1: 9). When we talk to the devil, we risk being led astray as Eve was (Genesis 3: 1–Our focus should be on God, not on demons; we talk to Him, not to them.

Life's greatest battles are not machine guns or bomb fights. We are all in a spiritual war. Human forces cannot win this war. We need the power of God. Spiritual warfare is between the forces of the devil and the army of God. Whoever loves Jesus will have to fight the enemy throughout life. But we are not alone. We are part of an enormous army, and our leader is Jesus! He gives us the strength to fight and win. God will destroy the devil's forces.

3

THE NATURE OF THE BATTLE

The Bible refers to the fact that we are soldiers; we are in a constant battle. Paul correctly declares that our battle is not against a person but against the spirit of the devil who is operating invisibly. What are your battles these days? There are some behaviors to prepare for to win the spiritual battle:

Recognize that there is an adversary: ignoring the adversary will not have positive results, and nobody wins a fight just by closing their eyes. The Apostle Peter urges us to be sober and vigilant; because our adversary, the devil walks about like a roaring lion, seeking whom he may devour (1 Peter 5.8).

Exercise the Authority that Jesus gave us: Jesus said that

we are peacemakers and that we live in peace. But the same Master also gave us power and authority over all demons and to heal diseases (Luke 9.1). This requires an attitude of war!

You need Armor: Going to war without protection is suicide. If by believing that you can win a spiritual battle just because speaking in tongues is a utopia. So, Paul says: *"Put on the whole armor of God, which you may be able to stand against the wiles of the devil"* (Ephesians 6.11).

You must shoot: Being armed "to the teeth" does not help much if I am not willing to use my weapons and shoot. Jesus assured us of victory by saying that everything we forbid on earth will be forbidden in heaven, and everything we allow on earth will be allowed in heaven (Matthew 16.19).

PRAY WITH YOUR WORDS

In Matthew 6: 7, we read: *"And when you pray, do not keep on babbling like pagans, for they think they will be heard because of their many words"*. Do you know that beautiful and pompous prayer that you heard from someone, and now you keep trying to pray like that person? Forget it: It is no use praying in beautiful words if these words are not sincere at first. When we pray, we must remember that, because of what Jesus accomplished on the cross, God is now our close friend. We should not see him only as an angry Creator, but as a loving father who wants to hear and relate to his children.

Praying is asking, searching, and knocking

When we pray, we can cast all our anxieties before God. This is what the apostle Paul teaches us in Philippians 4.6. Jesus said that we could not only ask but also seek and knock. This teaches us that sometimes we will have to persevere in prayer until the answer arrives. There are blessings that we will receive if we do not give up praying. You can receive a cure for anxiety, which is a terrible disease of the soul by praying and giving your worries to the Ones who can do everything.

God fulfills the requests of the warriors

In Joshua 10: 12-14, we read one of the most incredible biblical stories. Joshua was in the middle of a war against the Amorites. He dared to ask God for something unusual: *"Lord, make the sun and moon stop, while we are at war"*. The most incredible thing was not the daring of Joshua, but the fact that GOD answered and did what he asked.

When we are inserted in the wars of the Lord, when our hearts are in the kingdom's things, when our priorities are God's priorities, He supports us supernaturally.

We achieve impossible things through the prayer of faithful and bold leaders like Joshua. Prayer moves God's arm, but He has no interest in working miracles in the lives of those who do not want to serve Him wholeheartedly. Some people do not want involvement with the kingdom, do not want a commitment to God, and do not want to wear themselves out in the conquest of lives, but want God to answer their prayers. Joshua was legal to ask because he was involved in conquering the territories for the Lord.

The same will happen to you!

PRAY IN THE NAME OF JESUS

In John 14: 13-14, Jesus himself said: "And whatever you ask in my name I will do, so that the Father may be glorified in the Son. If you ask for anything in my name, I will do it". Some people when reading this verse, concludes that the name of Jesus is a kind of joke that, where a prayer is addressed to him that he might not answer it. This is untrue. See what it says in 1 John 5.14-15: "Now this is the confidence that we have in Him, that if we ask anything according to His will, He hears us. 15 And if we know that He hears us, whatever we ask, we know that we have the petitions that we have asked of Him". The prayer that is answered is one that is performed in accordance with God's will. He knows what is best for our lives, and it is for our care that he answers some prayers and fails to answer others.

What does it mean to pray in the name of Jesus?

It means praying, trusting in Jesus' merits, not in our efforts. When we ask for something **"in the name of Jesus"**, we are declaring: "Lord, I know that I am not worthy to be heard, nor to receive what I ask of you, but it is by trusting in the merit of your Son Jesus that I ask you this blessing and I believe that I will receive". Although it is lawful to pray to both the Son and the Holy Spirit, the most common form of prayer in the Bible is that which is addressed to the Father, in the name of Jesus, and by the power of the Holy Spirit.

Life is not an amusement park on a battlefield. Yes, we kill a lion a day (and even more)! And it will be like this until the last breath of life, when, in Christ, we will overcome our last enemy: death and its gods. To win, however, besides wearing all the armor of God (i.e., belt of truth, breastplate of justice, footwear of the gospel, shield of faith, helmet of salvation and sword of the spirit) - the word of God), as we are instructed by Paul (Ephesians 6.13-17), what we have to do, without losing strength, is to pray (Ephesians 6.18): *"Pray in the spirit at all times and occasions. Stay attentive and persist in your prayers for all the Lord's people"*. War prayer, therefore, is indispensable for our victory, both for the maintenance of our faith and for the advancement of the gospel among the nations.

As Christians, we should not seek the blessings of the flesh or try to get God to grant us more grace and blessings. These things only allow us to enjoy a worldly and transitory wonderful fortune, but they do not help us grow even remotely. Nor do they help us achieve faithful obedience and fear of God. Our prayers and supplications should focus more on our understanding of the truth, on putting God's words into practice and on growing in our lives. Only this prayer is in line with God's will.

When we experience difficulties, we must seek God's will and pray that we can testify and satisfy God. We must also have the determination to love and please God, to endure physical suffering if it means bearing witness to God, instead of praying for our own interests. Only that kind of prayer is in line with God's will, and that also means having the reason and conscience that we must have as created beings. Job, for example, lost all his possessions and children through his trials, and he himself was afflicted by wounds from head to toe. He suffered enormous physical and emotional pain. But he did not complain to God asking why He allowed him to suffer all of this, nor did he ask God to remove his suffering. Instead, he submitted first and prayed to seek God's will. He recognized that everything he owned had not been earned through his own work but had been given by God; it does not matter whether God gives or withdraws, as created beings we must naturally submit to God's government and arrangements. We must not make any demands or complaints to God. That is the reason that we must possess as humans. Job said: *"Naked I came from my mother's womb, and naked I will depart. The Lord gave, and the Lord has taken away; may the name of the Lord be praised"*(Job 1:21). Job ended up giving a resounding testimony of God by relying on his reverence, obedience and faith in God. We must learn from Job's example, and when we find something that is not in line with our notions, we must first quiet down before God and run and pray to seek God's will and pray that we can testify and satisfy God. This is the most critical aspect of our practice. In this way, God will guide us; He can give us faith and strength to help us get through whatever situation we may face so that we can stand on our testimony during trials.

4

WAR PRAYER

The Bible shows that there is a spiritual battle between the servants of God and the servants of the devil. It involves every believer in the spiritual battle. We must resist the adversary, but we need not be afraid of him, because God is stronger than all our enemies. The Bible says that our struggle is not against human beings. The proper battle is against evil spiritual forces that have authority over our world (Ephesians 6: 11-12). The devil destroys humanity, and he does not give up when a person is converted. Therefore, we need to be ready to fight (1 Peter 5: 8-9).

BE A PRAYER WARRIOR

Only those who do not trust their own strength can kill a lion a day, without being beaten on the way; they do not boast of past achievements; they do not allow the power to seduce or enslave themselves; the world, the flesh and the devil can only overcome those who, abandoning self-confidence, take refuge under the banner of Christ; cling to Christ's promises; pray with faith in Christ Jesus. Be a prayer warrior.

The difficulty of the Christian life is a reality, and the attacks of the evil powers are part of the reality for every child of God. Divine protection is also part of this reality. Therefore, resistance is done by constantly choosing to place oneself, by submission confident in his will, under the safeguard of the One who has overcome the devil and all those who serve him.

The devil's war against all of God's children is a reality. The devil's fury against Christ is carried over to those who follow Him. He could not overcome Christ; he takes revenge on those who are the object of his love. Therefore, the average Christian life is strewn with difficulties and traps, which can divert us from the essential: attachment to God and witness gave, both collectively and individually.

Prayers for spiritual warfare must be convincing because with them we aim to deal with demons and cast them out, making us the power of the Holy Spirit. Here we will teach you how to pray for spiritual warfare.

KNOW THE TACTICS OF THE ENEMY

We cannot be ignorant of the enemy's tactics. The devil is a conspirator, and a conspiracy is a plan, a ploy, or a program of action. However, we can defeat all the conspiracies of the evil one. The Bible tells us about the lurking of the devil (Ephesians 6:11); that is to say, their tricks, tricks, or the same: cheating.

War requires tactics and strategies; the generals must be excellent in those two aspects because you cannot win without a plan. Do not allow the enemy to strategize against you but defeat and destroy them through prayer.

The devil's traps and tricks are hidden, and people fall into them without even realizing it, but we can get rid of the hunter's trap, the soul hunter who is Satan. The way to be free and liberate others is prayer.

The enemy's key tactic is deception because he is a liar and the father of all lies. The Word of God shows us the enemy's tactics because God is light, and his Word is light, which can make the enemy visible and destroy the darkness.

The multitude is deceived by the enemy; there are hosts of lying spirits and deceivers who work under the authority of Satan. Spirits include illusion, deception, lies, seduction, blindness, error, and trickery. Our prayer can take power away from these deceiving spirits and make people's eyes open.

DAVID KNOWS HOW TO FIGHT THE DEVIL

David prayed against the conspiracies of his enemies; the psalms are full of references to the plans of the wicked to overthrow him. Still, his prayers were the key to destroying those plans and bringing liberation into his life. David prayed that his enemies would be scattered, confused, exposed, and destroyed. David's struggles were against flesh and blood enemies, but behind those enemies were spiritual entities who opposed his kingdom. Jesus was to come from the line of David and sit on that throne; therefore, David was fighting against something beyond the earthly. Through the Holy Spirit, David contended against the powers of darkness that were willing to fight against the coming of the Kingdom of God The powers of which we speak were also manifested through Herod, who attempted to assassinate the Messiah who was to come, moved by the spirits of fear and murder, and used by Satan to try to abort the coming of the Kingdom; however, the Holy Spirit had already been released through David's prayers and his throne was already secured.

Many of these war prayers were taken from David's psalms. Jesus, as the Son of David, sits on his throne, and the psalmist's prophetic prayers became weapons against the enemy's attempt to stop the seed that had been promised. David's victories in prayer opened the way for his throne to continue. The throne of evil could not defeat the throne of justice.

HOW TO FIGHT THE DEVIL

Any country, any army that wants to win a war, needs three essential things, which also apply to the spirit world: The front or attack, the rear or defense and protection, and the supply or support line. If the army is not prepared in these three aspects, it will surely be defeated.

For spiritual warfare, we see that many people have neither attacked, nor protected, nor supplied, which is why they are always defeated. Others only have the attack, the front line, leaving the rear vulnerable, the defense open. They have no supply. They scream and jump, but when the devil arrives, he overcomes them, because they have no weapons, strength, or power to fight.

Others have attacked, even protected, but they have no supply. They attacked the enemy's kingdom; they are protected, but they have no supply, and, over time, they are weakened. The devil waits for that moment to attack them. Other individuals have protection and supply. They don't lose. The devil does not beat them, but he is in a privileged position. He remains attacking and people defending themselves. They do not die, nor are they overthrown, because they have a supply, are being fed; they have protection, but they never experience victories because they only defend themselves. Satan is the one who goes on the attack.

5

TECHNIQUES TO CONDUCT A SPIRITUAL WARFARE

In a spiritual war, it generates the confrontation of spiritual powers. In this war, God manifests his power, his strength, his sovereignty through the church, and the clash is over Satan and all how he and his angels attack the world. In having to fight against the forces of evil and against Satan himself, the church must show its greatest faith, because it is, she who will show him the power and sovereignty of God, the church is his vehicle and must be prepared.

However, many people are prepared to attack the spirit world. In this war that you and I have fought, Satan leads countless demons. They are around us, trying to find a breach to reach us.

To win this war, we need to be attentive and vigilant and know the weapons we must use, besides some principles to be observed. Don't settle for small defeats, small losses, and small diseases. There may be an evil operation behind it all.

The devil knows how to work and is gradually arriving. He can never take advantage of us. Whenever you feel weak spiritually, it is a sign that the enemy is winning. Therefore, in the name of Jesus, decree war on him. Do not be afraid! Christ's authority is in you.

PREPARATION TO FIGHT THE ENEMY

In the army of God, we are his soldiers; we must improve our weapons and capabilities to remain in an excellent position of combat! Every soldier needs a stronghold, a safe place where he can fetch, treat, and restore strength. Our fortress must be our home. Our fortress must be spiritually clean, the peace of the Lord must take care of the environment; it must be a place where we can read, pray, and seek God! Be built up in God! But the devil will do anything to make his fortress a place of fight, disagreement among family members because while they are fighting among themselves, they will not be fighting against the devil.

God wants to pluck out of the Church all the spirit of fear or cowardice to bring a new encouragement towards new challenges, because when we are challenged to a life of more intense conquests, we are apt that, biblically. Let us attain the blessing that the Lord has prepared, both individually and collectively.

Now, we need to be aware that the hard thing for man is to enter a war without knowing the enemy's weapons. Jesus himself, in Luke 14: 31, 32, talks about this. We observe that every man must enter a war properly prepared or give a truce so that he is not taken by surprise. It is shameful for a man to both go and take his team to the battlefield if their weapons are not adequate. Many are said about the spiritual battle, but we notice a particular imbalance when it comes to the war in the spiritual world. Some simply ignore the opponent, which is destructive (it would be like a soldier being on the battlefield unconcerned about his enemy, he will inevitably be the first to die in the army).

Christ came to destroy the works of the devil:

"Whoever commits sin is of the devil; because the devil has sinned from the beginning. For this, the Son of God was manifested: to undo the works of the devil" (1 John 3: 8). When we make a prayer, it is personal communication with God; it is an intimate conversation in which we make God known for our needs and gratitude.

IDENTIFY YOUR WEAPONS

If we know the potential of spiritual coverage, we will prevent the devil from entering our borders, migrating through the gaps, or assaulting the edges. Prayer and Prophetic Acts are God's tools to keep us from being taken by surprise. In fact, it is a call from God not to allow the devil to enter our camp. For a long time, I have been meditating how we would improve the Church's role in conquering territories and preventing so many counterattacks plaguing our people. The answer came with the spiritual Rhema: Close the gaps through Prayer and Prophetic Acts. Today, better understanding the attacks we suffer, we are challenged to deepen the subject, which is inexhaustible. I believe that we will have vibrant experiences with God on the spiritual battlefield, which will contribute to the growth of the Body of Christ.

The entire Bible is full of conversations about enemies, battles, and metaphors about fighting. We must remember that it is a spiritual war in which we are engaged. We are fighting against *"... principalities, against powers, against the princes of darkness in this century, against the spiritual hosts of evil, in heavenly places."* Ephesians 6:12. This means that no matter how dark this world gets, no matter how tied to sin and iniquity the spirit of the world is, we are called to fight hard in the opposite direction. We are fighting for purity, for justice, for the will of God amid a wicked and corrupt generation. (Romans 12: 2; Philippians 2:15)

It is a life of action that every Christian should live. It is our job to prove that God's will is perfect. We must be at the forefront in the battle against Satan and the hosts of evil, who wish to have complete control over the world. We must be the obstacle that prevents them from achieving their goal: the last unbeatable barriers. The zealous supporters who prevent evil from taking over completely. We must be the light and the salt in this world.

(Matthew 5: 13-16)

The Bible, from Genesis to Revelation, teaches and encourages us to pray and exercise our faith. Knowing the depth of the Word of God, we see that the Lord instructs us not only to pray but also to do Prophetic acts, which are established by decrees and actions that, in the spiritual world, are determining factors for the possession of new territories.

Every individual who knows the Word of God should not underestimate spiritual matters and the clear teaching of the Scriptures. Our posture can send a message in the spiritual world, immobilizing the devil's action to release the church of God. You and I, as well as all those who want to exercise their faith responsibly, need to believe that there is a space of time that needs to be considered.

Satan is not retired, nor has he cooled down his projects, so the Church needs to know the potential of the Cross of Calvary and the teachings taught by Jesus to find out where all the solutions are for obtaining victory. Christ's death and resurrection are the remedies for all humankind, but the Messiah himself, before His death and resurrection, taught the Church how to defend himself against the devil's attacks.

To win faith is the key

May we unveil the principles of faith that will make us understand with higher sensitivity what exactly God wants from each one of us? Don't be intimidated! Advance! Optimize your faith and know who you are, because, by the plan of Redemption, we are more significant than we think, and we can do much more than we imagine.

DESTROY THE PLAN OF THE ENEMY

Jesus came to destroy the works of the devil (1 John 3: 8); these works are carried out by the forces of the enemy. Satan's kingdom consists of principalities, powers, rulers of the darkness of this age, and spiritual hosts of wickedness in the heavenly regions. There are different types of demons and different levels of evil. We can destroy the wicked tomorrow (Psalm 101: 8), and we can destroy those who hate us (Psalm 18:40).

Satan is rendered useless when his forces are destroyed, and we have the authority to bind the strong man and remove its weapons. The people of Israel were sent to destroy various nations, which carried the image of the world's kingdoms, each of which represented a different type of fortress that God wanted his people to destroy.

Demons are also represented by different creatures, for the diversity of the animal kingdom is an image of diversity in the kingdom of darkness. For example, the Bible speaks of snakes, scorpions, lions, jackals, calves, foxes, owls, sea snakes, flies, and dogs. These represent various types of evil spirits that work to destroy humanity. They are invisible to physical eyes but are nonetheless just as real as natural creatures.

We must always remember that there are more with us than against us. The forces of light are far superior to those of darkness. Jesus is the Lord of armies, and the armies of heaven are fighting with those of earth. Unleashing the angelic army is an essential strategy in war.

We can destroy the forces of darkness in the heavens, on the earth, in the sea, and under the earth. These forces can work through people, governments, economic systems, educational systems, and different structures established by men. These forces can operate from different locations and in different territories.

TOOLS TO FIGHT THE DEVIL

The Bible uses strong words when it comes to war, some of which are:

- Abolish: completely remove, cut, and pierce (Isaiah 2:18; 2 Timothy 1:10);
- Overcome: defeat, attack, grind, disturb, undo, thrive, terrify (Judges 9:45; 2 Kings 13:25; Psalms 18:42;
- Break: break, cut, crumble, dispossess, crush, smash, break (Exodus 34:13; Leviticus 26:19;
- Bring down: knockdown, deliver with the sword, cease, throw to the ground, throw, humiliate, make fall, trample, and cast into hell (Judges 6:28, 30; Psalms 17:13;
- Cast out: occupy by taking out the previous owners and possessing, cast, cast, cast before, vomit, cast out (Exodus 34:24; Mark 6:13; Revelation 12: 9);

- Persecute: follow with a hostile intention, flee, and drive away (Leviticus 26: 7-8; Psalms 18:37;
- Confuse: shame, embarrass (Psalms 35: 4, Jeremiah 17:18; 50: 2);
- Consume: perish, dissipate like smoke, stop being, and kill (Psalms 37:20;
- Contender: go to war, contend, defend, rebuke (Deuteronomy 2:24; Jude 9);
- Fight: dispute, contend, and fight (Daniel 10:20; 1 Timothy 6:12;
- Destroy: cast aside, abhor, punish, knockdown, ravage, uproot, exterminate, shake, pluck, ruin, kill, undo (Isaiah 23:11; John 10:10; 1 John 3: 8);
- Prevail: rise, strengthen, and strive (2 Chronicles Matthew 16:18);

PRAYER TO SET THE ENEMY IN FIRE

PRAYER POINTS

1. I extinguish with the shield of faith every dart of fire that the enemy throws at me (Ephesians 6:16).
2. I put out every dart of fire of envy, jealousy, anger, bitterness, and anger that is thrown at my life, in the name of Jesus.
3. I put out any blight sent by the enemy against my life, in the name of Jesus (Isaiah 7: 4).

4. I bind and rebuke any spirit of jealousy directed toward my life, in the name of Jesus.
5. I put out any fire that the enemy would like to cast in my sanctuary, in the name of Jesus (Psalms 74: 7).
6. I bind and cast out every fiery serpent thrown against my life, in the name of Jesus (Isaiah 30: 6).
7. I quench any spark of fire that comes from the mouth of Leviathan (Job 41:19).
8. The fire of the enemy will not burn me (Isaiah 43: 2).
9. I will pass any litmus test sent by the enemy against my life (1 Peter 1: 7).
10. The enemy cannot burn my harvest (2 Samuel 14: 30).
11. I put out all evil fire sent against my life, in the name of Jesus (Isaiah 9:18).
12. I put out every ungodly word spoken against my life, in the name of Jesus (Proverbs 16:27).
13. I extinguish any torch that the enemy wants to use against my life, in the name of Jesus (Zechariah 12: 6).
14. I put out all gossip directed against my life, in the name of Jesus (Proverbs 26:20).
15. The flame of the enemy will not burn upon me (Isaiah 43: 2).

PRAYERS AGAINST EVIL DREAMS

1. May all the arrows, wounds, harassments, oppositions, evil words, and decrees experienced in my dreams return backfires to the sender in the name of Jesus.
2. I reject any spiritual burden placed on my life through evil dreams, in the Name of Jesus.
3. Let all spiritual animals (cats, dogs, insects, spiders, snakes, crocodiles, or hideous beasts), who visit my dreams, be handcuffed and returned to the sender in the Name of Jesus.
4. May all my bondages related to evil dreams be changed to freedom, in the Name of Jesus.
5. Let all the losses suffered because of evil dreams be turned into advantages in the Name of Jesus.
6. Let everything negative that happened to me because of evil dreams be changed into positive actions in the Name of Jesus.
7. I arrest all spiritual attackers and paralyze their activities in my life in the name of Jesus.
8. May all the evil manipulations of my dream life, since my conception, be consumed in God's Fire in the name of Jesus.
9. May the Fire of the Holy Spirit locate and destroy any evil list containing my name in the world of darkness in the name of Jesus.
10. May all the arrows, wounds, harassment, oppositions, evil words, and decrees lived in my dreams be destroyed in the name of Jesus

11. May all the sufferings in my dreams be converted into triumphs and joys in the name of Jesus.
12. Let all the failures in my dreams be turned into success in the name of Jesus.
13. Let all bondage in my dreams be set free in the name of Jesus.
14. Let all the losses in my dreams since childhood be converted into gains in the name of Jesus.
15. May all war and opposition in my dreams since childhood be converted into victory in the name of Jesus.
16. May all physical poison in my system be neutralized by the Blood of Jesus in the name of Jesus.
17. Let every decree and evil mission declared against me by mouth be nullified and made void in the name of Jesus.
18. Let any of my spiritual problems attached to the hours of the night and the hours of the day be canceled by the Blood of Jesus and by the Holy Ghost Fire in the name of Jesus
19. I pull back my name from the registry of evil night restorers in the name of Jesus.
20. My father, my Father, may all my good dreams come true in my life by the Holy Spirit's power in the name of Jesus.
21. God, my Father, activate the manifestation of my good dreams by Your power in the name of Jesus.
22. I claim all the good things I lost through the attacks and the manipulations in my dreams in the name of Jesus.

6

PRAYER OF INTERCESSION AND SPIRITUAL WARFARE

Before you can be a successful intercessor, you need to learn to walk in victory and find an answer to your prayers. Don't worry so much about your level today. Start where you are, and the spirit will take you to step by step. As you expose yourself to Him and the Word, separating yourself to pray for others, He will take your hand, where you are now, and take you to an additional dimension, until you reach fullness.

Intercession means putting oneself in defense of another, it is done by crying out, interceding on behalf of someone, a church, city, or country, asking for God's help, with supplication and persistence.

To intercede is to put yourself in another's shoes and plead the cause as if it were your own. It is to be between God and men, in favor of them, taking their place and feeling their need so that they fight in prayer until the victory in one's life for whom they intercede. The intercessor is the one who goes to God, not because of himself, but because of others. He places himself in a priestly position (1 Peter 2: 9) between God and man, to plead his cause.

Let us intercede for all our families, for the people who work in the work of God, especially the servants of the Kingdom of God, who fight the good fight of faith, let us pray for each country in which you lived, let us do it using Biblical verses, Ephesians 3:10. Colossians 2:14, 15. In this end-time, it is necessary to be equipped and trained to pray with authority without fear. Those who know the Bible understand their duty to pray. Whoever devotes himself to the ministry of interceding, has a broader vision of the kingdom of God. He leaves his limited world and builds on his love and vision until he sees how Christ sees it.

When we devote ourselves to intercession, the world suddenly becomes our parish; we go up with Jesus, and the more you go up, the more you see. When you get stuck in your little kingdom, praying only for yourself:" bless me, Lord, me, me, etc... Lord, I have a problem". Jesus declared: When you begin to intercede, your heart will stretch to accommodate everyone. But if you are the type who only prays for your local church: Lord, bless sinners so they are converted and our Church is filled, your vision has the limit of your church. If you evangelize someone who is converted but does not stay in your church, you even think you have wasted your time. There are also pastors who curse church members who transfer to another church, as if the sheep were their property and not the supreme Shepherd of the church, Lord of the sheep, and all the folds that spread throughout the world.

In the book of Daniel 9. I observed that while Daniel was praying, a war was going on, his prayer that he had done from the heart, and was receiving a proposal. It is not at all like the famous spiritual warfare that many do. Let's cultivate the fruits more, the pleasant habits to give testimony and get along with God, or stay, and their cries will not do any good.

Who is an intercessor?

An intercessor who puts himself in the position of mediator for others who need a favor from God, gives their time to ask for help and favor from God on behalf of others. The intercessor dedicates time to pray for the need of others. Intercessory prayer is when we pray for other people that we assume with problems, needs, illnesses, etc., of other people, and we pray, beg, and ask for them, guided by love and mercy. An intercessor is a believer who feels the desire to pray for another, and takes his place, identifies himself with the pain of others, finds himself in communion with God the Father.

The intercession is a ministry in which Jesus is today involved in Heaven and the Holy Spirit on earth, and the believer is the channel of that intercession, we would dare to say that the idea of intercession is the incarnation of the virtues of the Lord Jesus. So, what qualities should the intercessor have? Now, since none of us has reached full maturity and we are all on the way, we are flawed in our intercession; however, with the help of the Holy Spirit and our diligence, we will grow, becoming an increasingly transparent channel of intercession, so that God may fulfill His purposes. Let me address some of the main characteristics of the true intercessor.

THE CHARACTERISTICS OF AN INTERCESSOR

It is defined as the ones who cry, recognize the needs, and bring them into God's presence. The intercessor is a person who loves God, reveres, honors, and worships God. He suffers from the pain of others; he does not want to see suffering in anyone; he only wants well for everyone; for this reason, he takes the burdens of others. He highly values salvation. That is why the greatest requests in intercession are to ask for the salvation of someone; other prayers will be for healing, for finances, for restoring marriage, children, for a change of character, for solving problems in a government or for going out to light all your deception.

The Lord Jesus example of intercession

Jesus Christ is the High Priest, is sitting at the right of His Father. The task that he takes care of as High Priest is to present himself before his Father in the name of his children, interceding for them. That is why the office of Christ as High Priest is to intervene. The subjects he negotiates are all that we need in our life to enable us to go to heaven - indeed, the Holy Spirit, who enlightens, consoles, and sanctifies us. We see this in John 14: 16-17: *"and I will ask the father, and He will give you another advocate to help you and be with you forever— the spirit of truth. the world cannot accept Him because it neither sees Him nor knows Him. but you know Him, for He lives with you and will be in you".*

The Lord Jesus, if he had not been a priest, there would be no salvation for the elect, because they have to come to God and be saved through a priest. For this reason, sacrifice and prayer go together. *"Who is he who condemns? It is Christ who died, and furthermore is also risen, who is even at the right hand of God, who also makes intercession for us."* (Rom. 8:34)

THE INTERCESSORS IN OLD TESTAMENT

- ➤ Abraham's persistent intercession for Sodom with Lot in mind (Gen. 18: 23-33)
- ➤ Moses' intercession on behalf of Israel (Ex. 32: 11-14; Num. 16: 20-22)
- ➤ Samuel's intercessory plea for the people (1 S. 7: 5, 8-9)
- ➤ Daniel, during the exile (Dn. 9: 1-19)
- ➤ Ezra, intercedes for restoration (Ezra 9: 6-15)
- ➤ Nehemiah intercedes for the restoration of his people (Neh. 1: 5-11).

WHEN AND HOW TO PRAY

Praying at all times with all prayer and supplication in the spirit and watching with all perseverance and supplication for all the saints. (See Ephesians 6:18). Above all, I urge that requests, prayers, requests, and thanksgivings be made for all men; for the kings and for all those who are in eminence so that we live quietly and restfully in all piety and honesty. Because this is good and pleasant before God our Savior, who wants all men to be saved and come to the knowledge of the truth. Because there is only one God, and only one mediator between God and men, Jesus Christ, (See 2 Timothy 2: 1-5) the duty of all of us who know the Bible and its truth, is to pray for those at home first, to beg for our brothers, for our nephews, cousins, uncles, brothers-in-law, for the entire generation and projection of our generation, asking first their salvation.

POWERFUL PRAYER OF INTERCESSION AND DELIVERANCE

Many times, we have asked ourselves, what can we do for our family, friends, or acquaintances, who have problems receiving the gospel of the Salvation of Jesus Christ? Other times, we Christians who find it difficult to pray, read the Bible, or serve the Lord. This prayer is ready to print and fill in the blanks with the name of the person we want to pray, or our name. God will do the rest. The only requirement: FAITH that moves mountains.

1. In the name of Jesus Christ, I tie the body, soul, and spirit of _____ to the will and purposes of God for your life. I bind the mind, will, and emotions of _____ to the will of God. I bind him to the truth and the blood of Jesus. I bind your mind to that of Christ that the very thinking, feeling, and purpose of Jesus' heart be within your thinking.
2. I bind the feet of _____ to the paths of justice, that his steps be firm and sure. I bind _____ to the victory that Jesus obtained for him (her) on the cross of Calvary, mercy, grace, love and forgiveness and dying to himself.
3. I untie and destroy every pattern of thinking, every attitude, idea, belief, habit, and motivation that is old. That does not come from God, knock them down, crumble them, and undo all ties associated with these things.
4. I untie and destroy any bondage in your life that is justified and holding a grudge against anyone.
5. I untie and destroy all lack of forgiveness, mistrust, and fear in him (her), in the mighty name of Jesus. I unleash and destroy the power and effect of deceit and lies on _____.
6. I unleash, in the name of Jesus, and destroy the confusion and blindness that the enemy has brought to _____'s mind, that has hindered him to see and understand the light of the gospel of Jesus Christ.

7. I demand the precious word of God, that seed that has entered the life of _____ that rises with power in him, because it is written: "GOD SENDS HIS WORD AND WILL NOT RETURN EMPTY" and "THE CANDLE OVER YOUR WORD TO FULFILL".

8. In the name of Jesus, I unleash and destroy the power and effect of all idle words, all criticism and negative gossip. I nullify and cancel all curse and blasphemy said by_____ or directed at him (her), or his marriage, family, or your ministry

9. I untie and destroy generational ties associated with _____.

10. I untie, destroy in the name of Jesus, all effect and bondage caused by some mistake that I made.

11. I crumble, undo and destroy in the name of Jesus all generational ties and mistakes made during past generations,

12. I destroy them now, at this moment, and from today they will never bind and curse the members of this family, in the mighty name of Jesus.

13. I bind the strong man, to enter his house and plunder all material and spiritual possession that he has stolen from _____.

14. I unleash and destroy the influence of the enemy on the body, soul, and spirit of _____.

15. I untie, I destroy, and I crumble every attempt of the evil one that the enemy wants to bring into his life this day. And I cry out that the Holy Spirit fills that void in (her).

16. I bind and untie in the name of Jesus. He has given me the keys and the authority to do so. Thank you, Lord Jesus, for your truth. Amen.
17. Once this powerful prayer has been performed, in your home, office, business or work, praise God and thank him with all your heart for the freedom that His beloved Son, Jesus Christ the King, brought us.

7

PRAYER AGAINST DEATH

God's will for all his children is that we live a very long and fulfilling life. Premature death is not God's will for us. In Exodus 23:25, God promised us we will live to fulfill our days (Psalm 91:16). He said that He would satisfy us with long life. Death is a certain destination for all living creatures, but God wants us to live a long and happy life on earth. Many of our covenant fathers who served God in the Bible lived very long and fulfilling lives. Abraham lived 175 years, (Genesis 25: 7), Isaac lived 180 years, (Genesis 35:28), Jacob lived 147 years, (Genesis 47:28). We serve the God of Abraham, Isaac, and Jacob, which is why we all may live a long and fulfilling life.

Below are Bible verses about our victory over death. These Bible verses will help us in our prayers to avoid premature death.

- Hebrews 2:14: For just as the sons are partakers of flesh and blood, he also took part in it; That through death he could destroy the one who had the power of death, that is, the devil;
- Revelation 20:14: And death and hell were thrown into the lake of fire. This is the second death.

PRAYER POINTS AGAINST PREMATURE DEATH

1. Every fear of death and slavery in my family is broken in the name of Jesus.
2. I declare today that no member of my family, including me, will live below 90 years in the name of Jesus.
3. I declare that old age will be synonymous with me and my generation in the name of Jesus.
4. Any calamity that makes people cry bitterly for me will not happen in the name of Jesus.
5. Oh Lord, I rebuke the spirit of premature death hovering around any member of my family in the name of Jesus.
6. Oh Lord, take my soul away from the grave and take my life away by the sword in the name of Jesus.

7. I decree and declare that God will fulfill every determined day of my life on earth. Father, I thank you because by faith I have in hand the divine order of restraint against premature death.
8. I will live and not die before my due time, and I will declare the great works of the Lord. Amen.
9. Any voice that calls me from the door of the grave is silenced by the blood of Jesus.
10. Powers crying out my name for destruction, your time is up, die in the name of Jesus.
11. I break the curse of premature death; owners of sadness and tragedy, carry your load and die in the name of Jesus.
12. I drink the blood of Jesus throughout my system.
13. Lord build the hedge of fire around me.
14. Spirit of life replaces the spirit of death in my life, in the name of Jesus.
15. I prophesy that every ploy of the devil and his agents to take my life will suddenly return fire to their heads in the name of Jesus.
16. I Decree that no matter what happens, I will not die before my time in the name of Jesus.
17. I declare today that any death covenant on my life is nullified and will not remain in the name of Jesus.
18. Curses to the demonic vessel and its network which the enemy would use to cause me spiritual wounds, in the name of Jesus.
19. Father Lord may Your glory cover all aspects of my life, in the name of Jesus.

20. Father Lord let Your angels camp around me in the name of Jesus.
21. I renounce, and I break every death covenant that I made, or that someone made in my name, in the name of Jesus.
22. I break any unnecessary alliance of premature death, in the name of Jesus.
23. All power, transforming into animals at night to attack me in dreams, fall and die in the name of Jesus.
24. Each coffin, prepared by the agent of death for my life, catches fire and burns to ashes, in the name of Jesus.
25. Every hole dug for my life by the agent of death, swallow the agents in the name of Jesus.
26. All powers, oppressing my life through death dreams, fall and die, in the name of Jesus.
27. All power of witchcraft, tormenting my life with the spirit of death, falls, and dies in the name of Jesus.
28. All power of witchcraft, assigned to my family by premature death, dispersal, and death, in the name of Jesus.
29. All satanic agents, who watch over my life in search of evil, fall and die in the name of Jesus.
30. Every unconscious gift of death that I have received, receives the fire of God, in the name of Jesus.
31. Each stubborn persecutor of my life returns and perishes in your own Red Sea, in the name of Jesus.
32. Every arrow of terminal illness come out of my life and die, in the name of Jesus.

33. Each power that imposes terminal illnesses in my life, falls and dies in the name of Jesus.
34. Every decree of premature death that hangs over my life sets fire and dies in the name of Jesus.
35. I reject and renounce all association with the spirit of death, in the name of Jesus.
36. All the inherited satanic glasses in my eyes are broken by the blood of Jesus.
37. Any ancestral agreement with the spirit of premature death, broken by the blood of Jesus.
38. Every agreement and pact of hellfire in the line of my family will be destroyed by the blood of Jesus.

PRAYER TO REMOVE THE HANDS OF THE DEVIL OVER YOU

1. I break their power against my physical and emotional health; I break them over my finances, overall activities, and tasks, so they cannot interfere.
2. I break them over my means of transportation, about my interpersonal relationships, about my perceptions so that do not confuse, on land, on my territories.
3. I order the evil forces to release my electronic devices. They will touch none of my objects to damage, steal, or destroy them.

4. I break them on my meters of light, gas, water, telephones so that they do not inflate them to increase my accounts, I order it in the name of Jesus.

5. The highest covenant that exists is the covenant of the blood of Jesus Christ voluntarily shed for me, I take refuge in protecting that covenant and renounce any other covenant practiced by my ancestors, by my enemies, that is binding me or harassing.

6. I order the demons invoked in these rituals to depart from me and those in my care, now in the name of Jesus, I send them bound to the abyss with the order not to return to us. God is my warrior, and He is powerful to keep me without fall (Jude 24), to keep me from your machinations. He is mounted on his white horse and has his sword ready (Rev. 19: 11-16).

PRAYER TO EMBARRASS THE ENEMY

I. Heavenly Father, I declare my loyalty and my surrender to you; You have sent me to free the captives; You have sent me to submit to You; You have sent me to resist the devil, and you have promised me he will flee from me. According to your word, I am on the warpath against the enemy; you have sent me to fight the good battle of the faith, and in your name, I advance against the enemy, making him retreat.

II. Lord, I take the offensive against the devil, completely confident in your authority and in your power to defeat him and crush him completely.

III. Get out of my family, out of my job, out of my house, out of my church in the name of Jesus out!!!

IV. Get away from me and those in my charge!!! Satan, now I order you to separate yourself from all of God's servants.

V. I cry out for the protection of God over all the people who have a ministry; I bless them with the protection of the Highest because His word promises that: "He who dwells in the shelter of the Most High will dwell under the shadow of the Almighty".

VI. Let my name be removed from any register of death by the Blood of Jesus, and I burn the evil records with the devouring fire of the Lord, in the name of Jesus.

VII. Any weapon of destruction forged against my family and me, be destroyed, wiped out by the Holy Ghost Fire of God in the name of Jesus.

VIII. Any evil gathering against my family and I, against our possessions, be dispersed by the thunder of the Lord's Fire! In the name of Jesus.

IX. O God, may Your devouring Fire destroy any evil list which contains my name and those of my husband / wife and children in the name of Jesus.

X. I paralyze any strong man attached to any area of my life. Be paralyzed! Be paralyzed! in the name of Jesus.

XI. I paralyze all the secret activities of family wickedness programmed in my life in the name of Jesus.

XII. Let all captivity be captive now by the Word of the Lord. According to Rev 13:10 I decree that "all the powers, the evil personalities who had planned to take me into captivity with my family, will go into captivity; those who kill by the sword, by invocations, bewitchments, evil words will be killed by their own works. This is the perseverance and faith of the family of the sanctified in Jesus Christ, of which I am a part! in the name of Jesus I declared!

XIII. Witchcraft hidden in my lineage, I order you, go out and die in the name of Jesus.

XIV. Any power of sorcery of the community that attacks education in my family, you are a liar, go out and die by fire in the name of Jesus.

XV. Any root of witchcraft in my family foundation, catch fire and burn to ashes in the name of Jesus.

XVI. Let every veil of ignorance in my destiny and in the destinies of my family members be swallowed and consumed by the fire of God, in the name of Jesus.

8

DECLARATIONS AND PRAYERS

It is an actual truth; the Holy Spirit leads the Church of Jesus Christ to a genuine confrontation with Satan. The fight is frontal and puts vast territories; God is on the offensive. We are winning the war. Hallelujah. This is a strategic war, with military strategies, places, and concepts keys to take and handle.

When we decree or declare God's Word, we are speaking life into our circumstances. We are announcing to evil forces, in high places, that God's Word has preeminence over what we see in the natural. As a result, God will cause our circumstances to change and come into alignment with His spoken living Word.

Before engaging the battle, it is crucial to start by this prayer as a password to defeat the enemy.

Dear Heavenly Father, I recognize I am a sinner who needs forgiveness. I confess Jesus is Lord. Your Son Jesus died on the cross for me, and you raised him from the dead. I renounce to the devil. I repent of my sins, and in the name of Jesus, I ask your forgiveness. Come into my heart and cleanse me. At this moment, I confess your Son Jesus as my Savior and Lord. Thank you for saving me. Amen

PRAYER TO CANCEL YOUR TERRIBLE PAST

1. I present before you my God; I enter your presence, and in obedience to your word, I prepare to receive your instructions, open my ears and my spiritual eyes, and baptize me in the fullness of your Holy Spirit. I am ready to learn from you. Lord, teach me to prophesy, teach me to discern Your voice, teach me to be your spokesperson to those whom you send me, I am preparing to receive your anointing on all the spiritual gifts that you want to make flow through me; I want to win everything you want to give me.
2. Father, I renounce pain and disappointment; I deny the insecurity that came from experiences in my past, made of the negative influence they have had on my life, and I put my trust in You.

3. I present to you every emotional wound in my life caused by people who have consciously or unconsciously damaged me, today I give you those wounds, so you heal them, heal my feelings, heal me from frustrations and heal me from brokenness.

4. I renounce all resentment against each person who has harmed me; I forgive everyone who has mistreated me and unleashed my hatred, triggered the desire for revenge, and the bitterness that has bound me to them in the past. I am free in Christ.

5. I renounce cowardice and indifference; I renounce deceit and lies and false prophecy; I renounce false vision and fake messages, subject the gifts to the Holy Spirit.

6. I do not accept receiving messages from any other spirit, whether human or demonic, I only receive the Holy Spirit's truth in the name of Jesus. Talk to me every day and teach me to catch your voice. To You be the honor, the glory, and the power forever and ever. Amen.

PRAYER FOR YOUR FAMILY PROTECTION

1. Lord God, direct me in this prayer for the sake of your holy name, cover me with your blood, cover my children, my family, all mine so that there will be no retaliation, nor winter transference on our life. Lord raise a wall on fire around us and prevent the evil attacks.

2. Beloved Father, protect us, Lord, from all evil and danger, take care of us with your sacred cloak and make us invisible before any threat or enemy that wants to truncate your plans.
3. Lord, destroy the principality of darkness that has destroyed our lives, homes, and ministries, all who have been the target of constant attacks of night, be surrounded, now, by your infinite protection, and deliverance, extend your right hand of justice, spread your wings of love over us, and hide us in your secret place.

PRAYER TO DESTROY THE WICKED

Enemies are beings that appear in our lives to be an obstacle stone in our way; they can be people, situations, or anything that fills us with fear, hopelessness, or affliction.

Our enemies can be anywhere: in our work, in our house, in our community, and worse still, they can be hidden from our view and disguise themselves as sheep when they are wolves on the prowl. To overcome them, we need all the help and strength from above.

> ➤ I destroy the strongholds of evil that insist on attacking us night and day, my God goes ahead, break the bronze bolts, and the iron braids, paralyze the attacks of the ferocious lion which it roars trying to destroy us, break its teeth, block the leviathan that destroys what is ours, paralyze the assaults of the

deceptive snake and curl it, that its distilled poison does not reach us.

PRAYER TO BREAK EVIL FORCES

1. Father, enter this furnace with us, act on our behalf, enter these lions' den, fall asleep one by one, take us out of this prison created by men whose heart is only perversity and deceit, break the iron rods, placed by Satan to prevent us from walking. God turns our captivity and shatters all the judgments that the evil one tries to put on our lives.
2. Father of mercy, act on our behalf, send your mighty angel to dethrone Satan and his principalities trying to destroy our lives; rebuke, all the spirits sent from winter to ruin our lives.
3. Lord arrive first, and throw down the altars of Baal, which are erected to confront us, shows that you are God in our life; let all the chains of darkness be broken, link by link, at this instant in the Name of Jesus.
4. Lord, I Rebuke Beelzebub, who has risen from hell, to destroy our family, our home, our ministry, and our life, that any spirit of prostitution, adultery, betrayal, manipulation of darkness, be banished from our midst, and cast into outer darkness.

PRAYER TO PARALYZE THE ENEMY

1. May, the spirit of deceit, lies and falsehood, aversion to the truth, condemnation, every spirit of suicide, which locks the mind and heart of some of ours, be destroyed at this moment in the name of the Lord Jesus.
2. May all the chains in this person's hands, feet, mind, and heart, now be broken, and that person has the escape coming from the Lord of hosts.

PRAYER TO NEUTRALIZE THE ENEMY

1. Father neutralize the devil that comes towards us, that every spirit of slander, envy, humiliation, insult, persecution, neglect, disrespect, of addictions, be neutralized in the name of Jesus, the Christ.
2. God, send fire from the high heavens and destroy everything that has wounded our hearts, making our souls sad.

PRAYER TO HUMILIATE THE ENEMY

Father of love humiliate those who have risen against our lives, unjustly, whether with us as you were with David, and shame those who slander us, those who have risen against us. Those mistaken in your house have a private with you, face to face, my God.

PRAYER TO DISMANTLE THE PLAN OF THE ENEMY

1. Father, rebuke the devourer, the locust, the destroyer, the rodent, the locust, the lizard, the scraps of hell that destroy what is ours, that all the nails of Satan now be crushed by your heel of fire, and what is ours, because you have already given us, be released now on our life.

2. Father, my Lord, we cry out in joy for the great blessings you have on our lives. Father, per your word, that you cannot lie, that according to these words that came from your throne to my heart, you make it happen. May the chains of hell fall to the ground, at this moment, the shackles of death be shattered, all impediments are destroyed, the bronze skies be annulled, and the glory of the Lord shines upon us.

CLAP YOUR HANDS TO CHASE THE ENEMY

Father in the one's name who has the name above all names, the Lord Jesus, the Christ Son of the living God, whose power extends for eternity, connected with your word that cannot go back, when I clap my hands together. Another three times, you enforce my petition before you, and everyone who reads this prayer and agrees, now receive your victory. So be it. Amen.

PRAYER TO COVER BY THE BLOOD OF JESUS CHRIST

1. Father in heaven, I yield in honor and adore you. I shelter myself with the blood of the Lord Jesus Christ as my safeguard during prayer.
2. I surrender completely and without reservations in every area of my life to the Lord.
3. I object against every work of Satan that may hinder me in this time of prayer, and I address only the living and true God, and I refuse any of Satan's involvement in my prayer.
4. Devil, I command you in the name of the Lord Jesus, leave my presence with all your demons, and I bring the blood of the Lord Jesus Christ among us.

PRAYER FOR GUIDANCE AND DIRECTION

❖ Heavenly Father, I praise and adore you. I recognize that the Lord is worthy to receive all glory and honor and praise. I renew my alliance with the Lord, and I pray that the blessed Holy Spirit will guide me during this prayer time.

❖ I am grateful, Father, for the love you have for me from eternity to sending Jesus Christ into the world to die in my place so I could be redeemed. I am grateful because He came as a representative and, through Him, the Lord forgave me completely; The Lord has given me eternal life; the Lord gave me justice perfect way of the Lord Jesus Christ so that now I can be justified. Thank you because, in him, the Lord made me complete, and because of the Lord offered to me to be my strength and help each day.

PRAYER TO CLAIM POWER AND AUTHORITY

1. Heavenly Father, come and open my eyes so I can see how great the Lord is and how complete is His providence for this new day.
2. In the name of Jesus, I take my place with Christ in heaven with all powers and powers (powers of darkness and evil spirits under my feet). Thank you for the victory that Jesus on the cross and at His resurrection. I'm sitting with the Lord Jesus Christ in heavenly places; therefore, I declare that all powers and powers and evil spirits are subject to me in the name of the Lord Jesus Christ.
3. Thank you for the armor that the Lord provided, and I put on the belt of truth, the breastplate of justice, the sandals of peace, and the helmet of salvation.
4. I raise the shield of faith against all the fiery darts from the enemy, and I hold the sword of the spirit, the Word of God, against all the forces of evil in my life, and I pray in complete dependence on the Holy Spirit.

PRAYER TO OVERCOME ACCUSATIONS

1. Thank you, Father, in heaven, because the Lord Jesus Christ overcame all principalities and powers and triumphed over them publicly. I declare all that won for my life now. I reject all Satan's insinuations, accusations, and temptations. I claim that the Word of God is accurate, and I live today in the light of God's word.

2. I bind and rebuke any false accusations right now, In the Name of Jesus! I acknowledge that every evil sponsor of my fake accusers shall go split from the ingrain in the name of Jesus.

3. Oh Lord, emerge and preserve me from those who speak terrible lies against me in Jesus's name.

4. I live in obedience to the Lord and fellowship with the Lord.

5. Lord, open my eyes and show me the areas of my life you don't like. Operate in my life, so there is nothing to give Satan an opportunity against me. Teach me any area of deficiency. Show me any space of my personality that I need to deal with to be more pleasing to the Lord.

6. Today I stand before the Lord so that the Holy Spirit will work in my life in how is needed.

7. Let every concealed enemy in my life, privately slipping out sensitive intelligence about me, be exposed, degraded, and demolished in the name of Jesus.

PRAYER TO CLAIM VICTORY

1. By faith and in dependence on the Lord, I dispose of the old man, and I receive the victory of the crucifixion that the Lord Jesus Christ provided for purification of my old human nature. I dress again, and I stand in the resurrection's victory and in what He provided for that I live out of sin. So, on this day, I strip myself of old nature with its selfishness, and I dress in the new life with God's love.
2. I strip myself of the old nature with its weakness, and I dress with the new character, which has strength.
3. I place myself in the victory of ascension and glorification of the Son of God when all principalities and powers were pointed to Him. I ask for my place in Christ victorious, with Him, over all my soul's enemies.
4. Holy Spirit, I ask that you fill me with your power. I destroy every idol and expel every enemy in Jesus's Name.

PRAYER OF SURRENDER TO GOD

1. Thank you, Father, in heaven, for expressing your will for my life daily, which the Lord showed me in his word. So, I claim all of God's will for today. Thank you because the Lord blessed me with many spiritual blessings in the places in Christ Jesus. Thank you because the Lord gave me a living hope through the resurrection of Jesus Christ from the dead. Thank you

because the Lord arranged for me to live today with the Holy Spirit's power, with love, joy, and self-control in my life.

2. I realize that this is your will for me, and therefore, I reject and resist all the plans of Satan and the demons to rob me of God's will.
3. Today I refuse to believe in my feelings, and I raise the shield of faith against all the accusations and all the insinuations that Satan tries to put in my mind. I claim the fullness of God's will for my life in Jesus's Name.
4. In the name of Jesus, I surrender completely to the Lord as a sacrifice. I choose not to conform to this world. I want to be transformed by renewing my mind, and I ask the Lord to show me his will and give me the conditions to walk entirely in it today.

PRAYER AGAINST FEAR

1. Heavenly Father, thank you because the weapons of our battle are not carnal, but mighty through God, to bring down strongholds spiritual, to undo all thoughts and attitude rise against the knowledge of God, and to bring everything in obedience to the Lord Jesus. So, in my life today, I take down Satan's powers, and I crush his plans against me.
2. I drop Satan's strongholds against my mind, and I give myself to the Lord, blessed Holy Spirit. I affirm, Heavenly Father, that

the Lord did not give me a spirit of fear, but of power, love, and sound mind.

3. I break Satan's plans against my emotions today, and I give my feelings to the Lord.
4. I crush the strongholds of Satan formed against my will today, and I give my will to the Lord and make the right choices of faith.
5. I crush Satan's strongholds formed against my body today, and I give my body to the Lord, recognizing that I am the temple. And I rejoice in His mercy and goodness.

PRAYER OF ASKING STRENGTH

Father in heaven, I ask that throughout this day, the Lord will alert me; show me how Satan is hindering, tempting, and lying to me, falsifying, and distorting the truth in my life. Help me to be the kind of person you like. Help me to be fervent in prayer. Help me to be strong mentally and to give you the right place in my life.

PRAYER AGAINST DISCOURAGEMENT

1. I protect myself with the blood of the Lord Jesus Christ and ask, may the Holy Spirit bring all the work of the crucifixion, all the work resurrection, all the work of glorification, all the work of the Pentecost in my life today, and I surrender to the Lord. I refuse to be discouraged. The Lord is the God of all hope. The Lord proved His power by raising Jesus Christ from

the dead, and I declare His victory over all active satanic forces in my life, I deny those charges, in the name of the Lord Jesus Christ with acknowledgment. Amen.

2. I decree and declare that because I have confessed all my sins and past mistakes, I am entirely forgiven! I order and claim that through Jesus, I am clean, free, and deliver!

SOME BIBLE VERSES TO USE WHEN PRAYING TO DEFEAT THE ENEMY

- **Revelation 12:9** – the great dragon was cast out, that serpent of old called the Devil and Satan, who deceives the whole world; he was cast to the earth, and his angels were cast out with him.
- **1 Peter 5:8** – Be sober, be vigilant; because your adversary the devil walks about like a roaring lion, seeking whom he may devour.
- **Luke 10:18** – And he said unto them, I beheld Satan as lightning fall from heaven.
- **James 4:7** – Submit yourselves therefore to God. Resist the devil, and he will flee from you.
- **2 Corinthians 11:3** – But I fear, lest somehow, as the serpent deceived Eve by his craftiness, so your minds may be corrupted from the simplicity that is in Christ

- **John 10:10** – The thief cometh not, but for to steal, and to kill, and to destroy I am come that they might have life, and that they might have [it] more abundantly.
- **Romans 16:20** – And the God of peace shall bruise Satan under your feet shortly. The grace of our Lord Jesus Christ [be] with you. Amen.
- **Ephesians 6:12** – For we wrestle not against flesh and blood, but against principalities, against powers, against the rulers of the darkness of this world, against spiritual wickedness in high [places].
- **Matthew 16:23** – But he turned, and said unto Peter, get thee behind me, Satan: thou art an offence unto me: for thou savourest not the things that be of God, but those that be of men.
- **2 Corinthians 4:4** – In whom the God of this world hath blinded the minds of them which believe not, lest the light of the glorious gospel of Christ, who is the image of God, should shine unto them.
- **Ephesians 4:27** – Neither give place to the devil.
- **Revelation 12:9-12** – And the great dragon was cast out, that old serpent, called the devil, and Satan, which deceiveth the whole world: he was cast out into the earth, and his angels were cast out with him.
- **John 8:44** – Ye are of [your] father the devil, and the lusts of your father ye will do. He was a murderer from the beginning, and abode not in the truth, because there is no truth in him.

When he speaketh a lie, he speaketh of his own: for he is a liar, and the father of it.
- **2 Corinthians 11:14** – And no marvel; for Satan himself is transformed into an angel of light.
- **Ephesians 6:11** – Put on the whole armour of God, that ye may be able to stand against the wiles of the devil.

9

CATEGORIES OF PRAYER

The Bible says that there are several categories of prayer. This means that the fellowship between the believer and God must not be just one way, like something cast and inflexible. If every prayer were the same, then there would simply be a systematic repetition of words, and God is not pleased with idle repetitions (Matthew 6: 7).

Prayer is a dialogue with God! An exchange implies a personal and complex interaction, and not just a script ready to be recited. In that sense, the Bible not only speaks of the many types of prayer in terms of their content, but it also speaks of the types of prayer in the sense of the many ways of praying.

It is necessary to pray that gives God legality for him to intervene in your situation. *"The highest heavens belong to the Lord, but the earth, he entrusted it to man."* PSALMS 115: 16. God only interferes if we ask. If we consider the entire biblical narrative, from the Old to the New Testament, we will see that there are many types of prayer. In teaching about the reality of spiritual warfare, Paul writes about the variety of kinds of prayer. He says that believers should put on the armor of God *"through all prayer and supplication"* (Ephesians 6:18).

Apostle Paul exhorts believers to use supplications, prayers, intercessions, and thanksgiving (1 Timothy 2: 1). Among the main types of prayer, we can highlight:

Thanksgiving prayer. It is that kind of prayer in which we dedicate ourselves to thanking God for all His blessings poured out on our lives, both physically and spiritually. We are usually very good at asking and terrible at thanking. So, let the thanksgiving prayer be more and more constant in our Christian life.

Petition and supplication. A petition prayer is that prayer in which we address God by presenting Him with all our needs. The Scriptures encourage us to cast all our anxieties on the Lord. We can do this with confidence, for He takes care of us (1 Peter 5: 7; cf. Philippians 4: 6). So, we can ask God for his provision by giving us daily sustenance and the things essential in our life; we can ask for spiritual blessings and gifts; for our guidance, protection and wisdom, etc.

PRAYER OF SUPPLICATIONS

1. Our Father, who is in heaven, I declare that you are my God. That I love you over all the people and things that exist. I love you with all my heart. I love you with all my soul. I love you with all my mind and with all my strength. Only you will serve you with all my strength. Only you deserve my adoration and my dedication.
2. God, you are the King of kings and Lord of lords. The throne of my life belongs only to you. My total dedication is to you.
3. I will serve no other god. You are my healer, my liberator, and my protector. You are the one who supports my life, the one who lifts me when I stumble. You are the one who encourages me when I feel discouraged, who trains my hands for battle. Yours is the kingdom, the power, and the glory, forever.

Intercession Prayer- It is the kind of prayer in which we intercede for other people. To intercede is to ask God on behalf of those around us or that we don't even know. This means that we can intercede for family and friends, but we can and must also intercede for people far from us. We can use this prayer to pray to God for our brothers in the faith who are scattered all over the world (Ephesians 6:18). Paul says that we should use this prayer to intercede for all men and made up authorities (1 Timothy 2: 1,2). We must pray even for those who mistreat us (Matthew 5:44).

Warfare Prayer: When you take the authority of Christ and exercise it over your opponent, you must be victorious. Many

Christians are oppressed by the enemy, unaware that their oppressor is Satan because the passivity in their prayers does not make a difference in the spiritual world.

The spiritual war is real, and you must train yourself, so you can fight it and be victorious. You cannot be asleep when you know that you have an enemy alert 24 hours a day, you must always be ready, prepared, to face your enemy and defeat him. That is why Jesus gave you the tools to face each battle and get rid of it.

WE ARE LIVING TODAY THE DAYS OF WAR!

"For we do not wrestle against flesh and blood, but against principalities, against powers, against the rulers of the darkness of this age, against spiritual hosts of wickedness in the heavenly places" Ephesians 6:12. We need to pray the prayer of war, the prayer that Moses said on the mountain, that David said here to overcome the enemies. Satan and his demons do not stop, so it is necessary to learn how to fight. *"Great deliverance He gives to His king, and shows mercy to His anointed, To David and his descendants forevermore"* PSALMS 18:50.

PRAYER TO START THE BATTLE

1. Father, in the name of Jesus, I dress myself according to your word with all the armor of God to face the tricks of the devil so that when the bad day comes, I can resist to the end with

firmness. I keep girded with the belt of truth, protected by the breastplate of justice and footwear with the disposition to proclaim the gospel of peace.

2. I take the shield of faith, with which I can extinguish all the burning arrows of the evil one, I take the helmet of salvation and the sword of the spirit, which is God's word.
3. I use these weapons of light to protect myself from all attacks by the enemy and advance in the name of Jesus against the kingdom of darkness. Now I anoint my body with oil to prevent any entry by the enemy. I anoint my family members with oil. I also anoint my animals.
4. I put the spiritual cover on myself, on my family, on the people are under my divine protection, I put a religious cap on my animals.
5. I raise God's fence on our means of transportation, on our material goods, and our works. I also cover the food we eat this day.
6. I cover my clothes and everything that comes into contact with my body.
7. I cover my ministries, spiritual gifts, abilities, and knowledge, so Satan and his demonic legions do not touch them.
8. I do not accept any attempt by the enemy to send us disease. I do not receive any of his curses for us. I do not allow Satan and his envoys to come and steal energy from us. I do not receive your plans to bring us accidents, destruction, or death. I do not receive kidnapping, abuse, or rape for us.

9. Now I anoint my house and all that you have given us, Lord. I anoint my car and invalidate every curse to cause an accident.
10. I do not receive the attempts of Satan to come to rob me. I cover the money and all the material goods that the Lord has given me against theft.
11. I do not receive the enemy's plans to harm me; I invalidate all evil plans to cause fires in my house, at my work, or while I am transported. I cancel any attempt to harm us through earthquakes, hurricanes, or floods.
12. I protect my home and my workplace from all curses sent for destructive purposes.
13. I declare that I am part of the Army of Jesus Christ, and I advance under his direction against any enemy, be it human or demonic.
14. I declare that the mighty hand of God guards and sustains me.
15. I declare the victory of the kingdom of God over the kingdom of darkness.
16. I declare that Jesus Christ defeated the evil hosts by voluntarily dying for the Redemption of humanity and by rising victorious.
17. I declare that before the name of Jesus, every knee must bow, and every tongue must confess that Jesus Christ is Lord. As a member of the war squad of the Most High God.
18. I command you Satan to submit to God's word and recognize the lordship of Christ over you.

19. I command you to bow to the one and Almighty God and confess that He is Lord, the only Lord and that He overcame you on Calvary's Cross. Kneel with your legions before Him and declare Him King of the Universe.

Advice to people practicing witchcraft.

I now turn to people who practice witchcraft to spy on or block the children of God. I warn you that the spirit of evil power will go back to your bodies. I forbid you to continue practicing the witchcraft, and I remind you that if you try, you will suffer physical and spiritual harm. It is better that you take advantage of this opportunity that the Lord gives you to repent and surrender to Him so you may enter the plan of salvation that He extends to humanity before it is too late. Know that Satan has deceived you by saying that you can no longer go overboard that is false. They are still on time. Repent of your sins, surrender to God and find a church where you can help free yourself from the demonic influence in your lives.

PRAYER TO CAST OUT DEMONS

1. In Jesus' Name, I cast out demons. I use Your Word, which is spirit and life, the Sword of the Spirit, more penetrating than any double-edged sword, able to discern the purposes of the heart, as a powerful weapon in You, to demolish the enemy

fortresses, to shatter them and dismantle their troops, in the Name of Jesus.

2. Under the authority of Jesus, my Lord, I resist the principalities, powers, and organized forces of evil in the heavenly regions.

3. Father train my hands for battle and my fingers for war. With Your help, I give a troop; I jump a wall with you. For you, train my hands for battle so that my arms bend a bronze bow. You have also given me the shield of Your salvation; Your right hand sustains me, and Your mercy magnifies me. You widen the path before me, and my feet do not slip.

PRAYER FIGHTING DEPRESSION

1. Beloved Heavenly Father, I come to You through Your Son Jesus Christ and, by the power of Your redeeming blood, I confess that I was negligent for all that time when I did not believe and did not trust in Your power of salvation and deliverance.

2. I ask forgiveness for all conscious and unconscious sins against You. In the name of Jesus Christ, Your Son, I ask you to forgive me for the sins I have committed. Clean me up, Lord! Purify me in your precious blood.

3. Lord Jesus, I ask you to have spiritual surgery and change the deceptive mental pattern. Lord, change my mind, renew it.

4. Lord, Sprinkle your blood, in the center of my soul, and free me now from the dark currents of depression, in the name of Jesus.
5. I authorize the Lord Jesus Christ to tie up all evil spirits and take them where Christ determines, and that they never come back in my life.
6. I now join Christ by His precious blood and give my mind to the power of Christ Jesus. Lord Jesus, pour out your precious spirit to heal the emotional wounds in my soul and enable me to forgive the offenders. I thank you in the name of Jesus Christ. Amen!

PRAYER AGAINST SORCERY AND HEREDITARY CURSES

1. Lord, God of our Lord Jesus Christ, I am confused; I do not know what to do in the face of so many losses, but in the name of Jesus Christ, I call for deliverance through His Spirit and His blessed Word.
2. I command all my fears, failures, traumas, hatred, revenge, and doubts to leave my life now, in the name of the Lord Jesus Christ.
3. I renounce all the words of the curse that have been spoken against my life and my family. May these curses not prosper and fall to the ground now, in the name of Jesus Christ.

4. I forgive those who hurt me, who hurt and deceived me. I pray and bless these people now. Lord, enlighten me by giving me understanding.
5. In the name of Jesus Christ, I break every evil force in my life, soul, mind, and will. I believe that I am free from all evil in the name of Jesus Christ. Amen.

PRAYERS TO OVERCOME SATANIC AND DEMONIC CONSPIRACY

1. I unleash confusion against all evil and demonic conspiracies against my life. May the secret advice of the wicked become foolishness in the name of Jesus.
2. Let those who have gathered against me disperse. Send your thunderbolt, O Lord, and scatter the enemy in the name of Jesus.
3. Destroy them, O Lord, and confuse their tongues (Psalm 55: 9). No weapon forged against me will prosper, the gates and plans of hell will not prevail against me.
4. I defeat all the strategies of the devil against me in the name of Jesus.
5. Every strategy from hell is exposed and brought to light. I receive God's plans for my life, thoughts of peace, and not of evil in the name of Jesus

6. I am free from all traps and plans of the evil one against my life. I unleash the whirlwind to disperse those who conspire against me in the name of Jesus

7. I order that all monitoring spirits, strategies, human vessels, and positions of contact be denied access to our lives, loved ones, finances, and records. I concede that every monitoring quality and vessel be confounded, desensitized, and permanently displaced from every aspect of our lives.

8. I command that every satanic or soulish mark placed on us in the spirit, be washed away by the Blood of Jesus and that all our garments be changed to new, spotless, radiant garments fitted for our prophetic purposes.

9. I command divine order to be established in every dimension of our lives and the church's life. I call for the spirit of good stewardship and excellence to be activated in our lives and the lives of all church leaders and members.

10

PRAYER AGAINST GENERATIONAL CURSES

If you or any of your ancestors gave way to demonic entities, your family might be under the "Hereditary Curse", and it will pass this on to your children. Every sin has personal guilt but a collective consequence. Let's say again that, "your father was an adulterer" that opened a gap for his demonic possession and his marriage and gave legalities for the entities to be working in this area of his life, so his sin was not repented, so no has been redeemed, so these demons or entities, they continue to work in his life and the one's family who sinned.

When attending consultations with a health specialist, they usually ask if we have any family members with transcendent problems. Many diseases are part of this punishment allowed by God; only a few are cancer, arthritis, and diabetes. But as already mentioned, not only do they manifest themselves in well-being complications, they can also have a family cycle in which accidents or tragedies occur.

Vices likewise pass from generation to generation; one of the best known is alcoholism; coupled with this aggressive facts, premature deaths and economic poverty accompany this condemnation. It causes them because an ancestor of our bloodline crossed the wall of sin, taking part in some sect related to the occult and witchcraft. As a result, the well-being of the following generations is affected by the evils already expressed.

THE SIGNIFICANT OBSTACLES TO PRAYERS

Before beginning any prayer in Spiritual Warfare, EVERYONE in the family must commit not to speak complaints, insults, criticism, shouting, claims, defeat, bitterness, but to CHANGE the familiar language of a curse to BLESSING. Lawsuits, screaming, strife, disagreement, and bigotry must go away FOREVER from home; otherwise, everything will be a monumental failure. From now on, the language will be changed to BLESSING language, and God's victory will be declared in everyday language. If the atmosphere of litigation and strife and bitterness continues in the home, PRAYERS WILL DO

NOTHING. Having negative, pessimistic, or cursed word can undermine your prayer.

Christians who pray to God for a situation and declare victory and then later express negativism, bitterness, pessimism, defeat, curse, and their everyday language will NEVER see their prayers answered. Therefore, for years, there are many Christians who pray for a situation that is never resolved. The language we used to pray must be in concordance with our everyday language.

IMPORTANT PRAYER POINTS

1. Heavenly Father, I come on behalf of my generational line and behalf of my life. I acknowledge your commitment that "no weapon formed against me will prosper, and every tongue that rises against me in judgment will be sentenced." I recognize your word that if we erroneously conclude or censure without sympathy, we will likewise be judged or convicted.
2. Holy Spirit, I ask you to help me examine my heart so I can see and remember my judgments towards other Christians. Help me make a list of the people I hurt and even those who didn't know about my criticism or condemnation.
3. Heavenly Father help me find and remove all bitter thoughts and judgments, statements that hurt other people's hearts and remove all curses I have spoken, including all associated prayers that were not according to Your will.

4. Father, I repent for those we curse and murder with our words of vengeance, slander, gossip, and ungodly judgments, in the body of Christ, including negative declarations of need, zero prosperity, and condemnation of other Christians, and especially against members of our own family.
5. I especially repent for those judgments made from our leadership positions within your body as pastors, teachers, apostles, prophets, and evangelists, defensively justifying ourselves for some received offense, or jealousy, or some controversies in doctrine and confusions. Lord, we have sinned with our speeches and opinions, invoking curses and opening the door to consequences on ourselves and others' lives. Please, Lord, forgive us.
6. In the name of YESHÚA I break every curse that comes into my life, for these sexual relations and I bind and cast out all the demons they minister these curses, they are leaving now, in the name of YESHÚA.
7. I renounce and resist Satan, the ancient serpent, and all its hierarchies in the name of Jesus.
8. I renounce and resist Diana of the Ephesians, I renounce and resist Sheva.
9. I deny and resist Asmodeus, Beelzebub, Baal in the name of Jesus.
10. I renounce and resist Mammon. Everyone now leaves my life, my mind, my body. They are leaving now with all their demon hierarchies!

11. Out now, in the name of Jesus! I resist all of you now, and I will no longer give you a place in my life! I tie you up and throw you out of my life and leave now in the name of Jesus.
12. I break every curse and covenant that Satan has contracted to steal, kill, and destroy me in the name of Jesus of Nazareth.
13. I break any curse of theft of death and destruction spoken against me from any person, friend, client, family, children, and parents in the name of Jesus of Nazareth.
14. I break every curse of fornication, adultery, sexual abuse, unnatural sex, illicit sex, illegal sex, bestiality, homosexuality, masturbation, lesbianism, succumbing, and in succumbing made by my previous partners and me in the name of Jesus of Nazareth.
15. I break all spiritual blindness of my understanding made by the God of this century in the name of Jesus of Nazareth.
16. I break and nullify every covenant, oath, and impious promise that I have made with my lips in the name of Jesus of Nazareth.
17. I renounce all curses of pride, greed, poverty, scarcity, sadness, the pain of my ancestors that influence my life in the name of Jesus.
18. I renounce all family spirit and guiding spirit that wants to work in my life from my ancestors in the name of Jesus of Nazareth.
19. I renounce all false beliefs, religion, myth, philosophy, dogma, paradigms, rites, heresies, and all impious and evil belief systems in the name of Jesus of Nazareth.

20. I renounce and break any impious oaths made by my ancestors to idols, demons, false religions, and impious organizations in the name of Jesus of Nazareth.

21. I renounce all unclean spirit of idolatry, adoration of images, faith in images, faith in myself, faith in men, faith in the demons that work behind the pictures of the name of Jesus of Nazareth.

22. I renounce all unclean spirits of witchcraft, sorcery, divination, and occultism, Freemasonry, yoga, hexes, spells, magic, hexes, charms, and hunches in the name of Jesus of Nazareth.

23. I break all curses and negative words I have spoken against my life, my family, and my children in the name of Jesus of Nazareth.

24. I break any curse and negative word that has been spoken about my life by other people, including those in authority, in the name of Jesus.

25. I break all yoke of ancestral spirits of Freemasonry, idolatry, witchcraft, false religion, polygamy, lust and perversion that operate in my life in the name of Jesus of Nazareth.

26. I break all the ancestral spirits of lust, rejection, fear, discomfort, weakness, illness, anger, hatred, confusion, failure, and poverty that operate in my mind and heart in the name of Jesus of Nazareth.

27. I break all legal rights of all generational spirits operating in my soul behind a curse, destruction, and death in the name of Jesus of Nazareth.

28. I break any curse on my economy that comes from my ancestors who have cheated or mismanaged money in the name of Jesus of Nazareth.
29. I break all curses of discomfort and diseases in my body inherited from my ancestors in the name of Jesus of Nazareth.
30. I break all oaths, vows, covenants, curses that my ancestors have done with the devil against me in the name of Jesus of Nazareth.
31. I break every curse made in secret against my life by agents of Satan, in the name of Jesus of Nazareth.
32. Lord, thank you for restoring me to my role of dwelling as your son or daughter as I collaborate with you to break all the curses that were invoked.
33. I take my authority in the name of Jesus, sitting next to You, I declare that the kingdom of heaven has approached to dismantle, break, destroy, and demolish all curses we have sent, and those that were sent to us.
34. I also declare that no weapon forged against my life will prosper and that every enemy that stands against me in judgment is now condemned and thrown out.

WARFARE PRAYER TO GET MARRIED OR TO KEEP YOUR MARRIAGE

Marriage is an institution ordained God. It is God's will that you marry. The Bible says that his companion will not be lacking, (Isaiah 34:16). Every delay in your marriage is not God's will; therefore, today, we will take part in warfare prayer to get married. As we bet, this spiritual warfare prayer God will connect you to your destined husband/wife in the name of Jesus. God can never be late, no matter how old you are now or how many years of your companions, just trust God.

Do not measure your life according to the time of other people, rather wait to the Lord in prayer, and He will take you to your land of married happiness in the name of Jesus. Marriage is not an institution you rush to; you must prepare yourself in prayer for it. It is a spiritual adventure. Many people have rushed to get married just to get divorced. This is very sad. A damaged relation is often more reliable than a troubled marriage. You must explore the encounter of the Lord concerning your marital destiny. You must ask Him to direct you to your God-ordained spouse, and God will lead you. God is your Creator and your maker. He knows the best man/woman for you. When you look for his face before marriage, He guarantees your marital happiness.

You must also pray against the forces of darkness, seeking to delay your marriages. The devil has put satanic veils on the faces of many singles and spinsters today, preventing them from getting married. Still, as we perform these spiritual warfare prayers to get married, all satanic spells in your life will be destroyed forever in the name of Jesus. *"But I want you to know that the head of every man is Christ, the head of the woman is man, and the head of Christ is God"* 1 Corinthians 11:3.

STRATEGIC PRAYERS

1. Lord of Hosts, in the name of Your Son Jesus Christ, I come in your presence to ask you to give me a full understanding of my mission, which is to assist my natural husband, and Christ, my spiritual husband, who are the authorities over my life.

2. By the power of His resurrection, I disconnect myself from all rebellion now, and through His blood, I join Christ to express His virtues.

3. Lord, give me the perfect vision of the ministry of submission so that your intentions may flow through me to be a blessing in married and ministerial life. Allow me to discern the opportune time to bring food to the king and recognize God's anointing. I praise You and thank You, Heavenly Father, for eternal life and the opportunities you have given me to know Your authority. Amen.

4. Lord, have mercy on me, forgive me of all my sins and cleanse me of everything injustice in the name of Jesus.

5. Father let your sword of liberation heal me and rescue me from all matrimonial slavery in the name of Jesus.

6. Every evil spirit of the valley, moving in my way of life against my family and marriage, fall and die in the name of Jesus.

7. Any ground that you have lost to enemies through sexual perversion will be withdrawn in the name of Jesus.

8. Oh Lord, open a path for me in my marital destiny while I work before you in the name of Jesus.

9. Strong man of my father's house, where is your victory? You could not retain the Lord Jesus Christ. You are not going to stop my marital advances in the name of Jesus.
10. Father God let me receive Your divine mercy and favor in the name of Jesus.
11. By the blood of Jesus Christ, I free myself from any form of a parental curse that is imposed on me consciously or unconsciously in the name of Jesus.
12. By the blood of Jesus Christ, I renounce every evil spiritual marriage in the name of Jesus.
13. Let the blood of Jesus, wash me in the name of Jesus.
14. Any power that attacks me as a result of this prayer will fall and die in the name of Jesus.
15. Holy Spirit fire falls on me, burns in my body, soul, and spirit, in the name of Jesus.
16. I denounce any evil association of family spirits, in the name of Jesus.
17. I break all barriers between my partner and me, in the name of Jesus.
18. I declare a spiritual connection between my God-ordained spouse and me in the name of Jesus.
19. I reject the forgery of the devil. I receive the original from God today, in the name of Jesus.
20. I reject and renounce all curses against marriage that my parents issued to me.

21. By the power of the blood, I command the strong east wind of God to remove all distractions and obstacles that Satan frequently uses to block my companion.
22. Lord forgive me all my sins and those of my ancestors, in the name of Jesus.
23. By this Prayer, Lord, I divorce my own will to receive the will of God.
24. By Your zeal, God of Ruth, send me help in the name of Jesus.
25. You, God of acting, do what no man can do for me in the name of Jesus.
26. By the blood of Jesus Christ, I wipe out all dreams of swimming in the water, eating strange foods, having sex in the name of Jesus.
27. I acknowledge that the seductive power of the Holy Spirit will draw my God-ordained spouse to me now in the name of Jesus.
28. I am separated by fire from every unprofitable relationship in which I am now in the name of Jesus.
29. I release myself from the husband/wife spirit in the name of Jesus.
30. I declare this year I will be gloriously married in the name of Jesus.
31. Heavenly Father, thank you for answering my prayers in the name of Jesus.
32. I solicit the Blood of Jesus over any sins perpetrated by our parents and ancestors. I cut through the Blood, any satanic

covenants, protocols, networks, promises, or agreements conducted over our lives, bodies, souls, and crises.

33. I acknowledge that I am redeemed FROM the control of the Devil by the Blood of Jesus. I insist that all satanic thrones, altars, dominions, territories, rulers of darkness, spiritual hosts of degradation, and all wicked works have no jurisdiction over me. I claim that satanic harassment and intimidation have no effect on us.
34. I order that every cover of the enemy shall be removed out of our ways of life and the lives of our loved ones. I end all satanic projections, fiery darts, projectiles, witchcraft activities, and soulish prayers.
35. I acknowledge as it is written, my prophetic destinies and purposes will be fulfilled now without delay.

PRAYER FOR JUSTICE

1. Lord God, in the name of the Lord Jesus Christ, I now put on the breastplate of justice.
2. I repudiate any dependency I may have of my own free will. I embrace the justice that is mine by faith in the Lord Jesus Christ.
3. I count on the Holy Spirit to carry out acts of justice, pure thoughts, and holy attitudes.
4. I raise the banner of the righteous life of the Lord Jesus Christ to defeat Satan and his kingdom.

5. I claim that my victory is obtained and lived by my Savior.
6. I ask anxiously, and I am confident that the Lord Jesus Christ will make His righteousness live through me. Through the precious blood of Christ, cleanse me from all my sins of omission.
7. Make me walk in a holy and right way so that I will honor God and defeat the devil and its agents through Jesus Christ, my Lord. Amen.

PRAYER OF VICTORY

1. Merciful Heavenly Father, I choose to see myself as You see me in the person of Your Son, the Lord Jesus Christ. I prefer to see myself as someone invincibly strong to accomplish everything in Your plan for me.
2. I reject Satan's accusations that I am irredeemably weak and defeated. I accept my present great difficulty as a call to renew my Lord's vision of victory.
3. Help me focus my attention on the majesty, power, and sovereign greatness of my Heavenly Father, who cannot fail.
4. Help me see that in my union with Christ, I am more than a winner, that the burden of my trials becomes a manifestation of the Lord's responsibility. May this burden manifest itself in tears of worry, hours of fasting, and prayer.
5. I choose not to shy away from the burden. You want me to carry.

6. I recognize Lord that it is mainly my sin and my failures that brought this intense trial.
7. I deeply regret my sins of.......... (name each of the mistakes you realize you make). Clean me in the blood of my Savior.
8. I take back from Satan all the land that I have given you with my sins and transgressions, with the authority of the cross, I claim all that land for the Lord Jesus Christ. Precious Lord Jesus Christ, you promised me never to leave or abandon me. I know this is true, and I boldly say: "the Lord is my helper; I will not fear". Firm in the faith, I resist the devil and his kingdom.
9. I command Satan and his demons to leave me and go where the Lord Jesus Christ sends them.
10. Heavenly Father, I accept and enjoy all that is written on the scroll of Your will for me.
11. Thank you because I can do all things in Christ that strengthens me. I will do Your will, accepting my responsibility to be reliable, I will do with Your strength what I know to be Your will.
12. Thank you, Beloved Heavenly Father, because through the Lord Jesus Christ you have heard my prayer and will make me walk like someone so strong in the Lord, that even Satan's most potent strategies will already be defeated. I pray in the name of the Lord Jesus Christ and for Your glory. Amen.

PRAYER OF PROTECTION

1. I declare the protection of the belt of truth about my life, my home, my family, and my work, which God has established for my family and me in the name of the Lord Jesus Christ.
2. Let the belt f truth be directed against Satan and his kingdom of darkness. With determination, I embrace the one who is the truth, the Lord Jesus Christ, as my strength and protection against the deception of Satan.
3. I ask that the truth of the Word of God take a higher place in my life.
4. I pray that my heart can delight in studying and memorizing the truth of God's Word.
5. Forgive me the sin of not speaking the truth, show me if I am being deceived in anything.
6. By the Holy Spirit of Truth, open my understanding to the Scriptures and lead me to an understanding for the practice of His Words of Truth.
7. Thank you, Lord, for the ministries of Christ, a stronghold for Your Truth in my life, help me to integrate myself into the body of Christ, and have full communion with the brothers in Christ.
8. I understand, Lord Jesus Christ, that the ability to be invincibly strong and to carry out Your determination compels the sustaining power of the belt the truth Thank you for granting this piece of divine armor for my life, I thank you.

11

PRAYER AGAINST JEZEBEL SPIRIT MANIPULATION AND CONTROL

We, as churches, consistently live in a spiritual battle, suffering attacks from all sides. That is why Jesus warns us we must live continually watching and praying, so we are always ready. Besides studying the word of God (the Bible). Jezebel is well known for her hatred of prophets. Jezebel's actions were so intense against the people of God that an evil spirit of world influences that acts for destroying God's authority adopted her name. I thank God for the revelation given to me, who can scrutinize, with authentic examples, all the actions of this spirit in the church.

A person with that spirit feels persecuted. They are always telling people what they have done to them, how unfair, that there is no appreciation for them, and they do all this to make them feel sorry and compassionate. Through self-pity, this person controls and manipulates the family. Often, she/he is bitter, especially towards men, their father, and even other authority figures.

People with Jezebel spirit don't submit. They cannot tolerate being told "no" because they are preparing for war. Jezebel is always contending and speaking against those in authority. She/he hates the prophets and the church prayer because they discover it. She/he likes nothing that has to do with prophecy because she/he is directly confronted and located. Have you ever felt insecure? Jezebel wants to move into an environment of insecurity, frustration, and confusion. Jezebel loves power and control.

What are the targets of this spirit in the church?

Pastors, evangelists, influential leaders, worship and worship leaders, and intercessors.

Jezebel's spirit will destroy any church that has a revival, revealed word of God, and a fresh and continuous anointing of the Holy Spirit. They manipulate children and use them as a manipulation tool. Our defense is repentance and liberation; it is to live with a clean heart. It is noteworthy that genuine repentance produces real divine intervention and presence in the person's life in need.

PRAYER POINTS

1. Lord Jesus, I give permission to the Spirit of Life to command the Lord's angels of war and fight the spirits of self-righteousness, manipulation, and control.
2. I release Your anointing to remove all the ideas, projects, and feelings that Satan has kept in my heart in the name of Jesus.
3. I now allow, by the power of Jesus' name and blood, that the angels of the Lord are sweeping these demons with the fire broom of God into the depths of the abyss.
4. Lord, arrest them, do not allow them to manifest themselves in my mind anymore to express themselves and do evil throughout my life.
5. I want to consecrate my mind and heart to Jesus Christ and the Spirit of Life in the name of Jesus.
6. Lord Jesus, You are free to operate with power and authority to sweep from my heart all that is of darkness because I was created to be a vessel of God, and I want today to make this vessel available, which I am, for the exclusive use of God.
7. I now order Jezebel's manipulative spirit to be dethroned and wholly detached from my soul in the name of Jesus.
8. I thank God that the flow of the spirit and the anointing within the spirit are now taking command of the hands of the spirit of Jezebel.

9. May the Spirit of Life rule and reign over my soul from today onwards because Christ's blood has already freed me from darkness. Jesus Christ, my Lord, whom I will follow to the end; this is my freedom. Amen.
10. Out now Jezebel, you will not hold me captive anymore in the name of Jesus.
11. The Holy One of Israel is shouting liberation around me. He rises like a mighty Giant and crushes you under my feet in the name of Jesus.

PRAYER AGAINST MANIPULATION AND REJECTION

1. Lord Jesus, at this moment, I open my heart to receive Your Word with meekness. May, all the spirits of the old man, who make up the body of sin, and still influence my soul, be removed from me.
2. May all be subdued by the power of the blood and the name of the Lord Jesus. I declare that I am open to receive the revelation that there is a divine life is in me.
3. Lord Jesus, I reject the spirit of disobedience, seduction, manipulation, rejection, and idolatry.
4. I renounce and resist being a person who controls and meddles.
5. I renounce and resist manipulation and domination.

6. I renounce and resist using sex as a weapon of punishment or revenge or to negotiate things.
7. I will never have lovers. I renounce and resist lust and lust.
8. I renounce and resist the spirit of prostitution in the temple.
9. I renounce and resist the spirit of the dog.
10. I declare the spirits of disobedience, seduction, manipulation, rejection, and idolatry tied up.
11. Father God, I overturn, override, and block the spirits of disobedience, seduction, and Jezebel tries to interfere with my destiny in Jesus's Name.
12. Lord Jesus, forgive me because I have made myself a false god. Lord Jesus, I will accept the circumstances You have sent to me because I know that You are giving the treatment for me to be built up in the inner man according to God; so I can become a king and a priest as Your purpose is. I am open to this work. Amen!
13. I acknowledge that perfect setting, important relationships, open doors, and favor in high places shall manifest continually.
14. I command divine solutions for every trouble in our lives to reveal. I request every satanic mystery, cycle, and mechanism to be permanently exposed, decoded, and consumed through the Blood of Jesus.
15. I acknowledge that every legality, technicality, ordinance, and decree issued against us in the spirit's domains be overturned. I command an embargo, and governing order be

issued AND ENFORCED against all acts of injustice and molestation. (Colossians 2:14)

16. I acknowledge that God will prevail in our favor, and the divine order for our rehabilitation be implemented and be cleaned away, and I will collect double honor.

17. I acknowledge that I switch on the Blood of Jesus to plead i authority working behind the scenes. (Revelation 12:11)

18. By the power of the Holy Ghost, I acknowledge that they are bound, and all of their guns are destroyed. I command that Satan's ground troops, individuals without bodies and human vessels be seized, robbed of their authority, deadened, and permanently disorganized.

19. I release the LORD's blessings to locate and overtake us in every circumstance, business transaction, relationship, and everyday activity. I acknowledge that goodness and mercy shall follow us all the days of our lives, and I shall never depart from the House of our LORD.

12

DIVINE HEALING
PRAYER FOR ALL TYPE OF SICKNESS

Almighty God, in the name of the Lord Jesus, I praise You for the victory I have in Christ Jesus because I am free. After all, the Son of God has set me free. Thanks to Him today, I am seated with Christ in heavenly places, above all principality and all power.

1. Formidable and marvelous are your works, that my body works wonderfully for which you designed it.
2. The sacrifice of Jesus of Nazareth on the cross is the legal right that I am healed of all diseases.

3. My meat will be fresher than that of a child, and I will return to my childhood days.
4. I cast out every unclean spirit of affliction that attacks my body in the name of Jesus of Nazareth.
5. I cast out every unclean spirit of disease that has entered my life through pride in the name of Jesus of Nazareth.
6. I cast out every unclean spirit of ailment that has entered my life through trauma or accident in the name of Jesus of Nazareth.
7. I cast out every unclean spirit of disease that has entered my life through rejection in the name of Jesus of Nazareth.
8. I cast out every unclean spirit of disease that has entered my life through sorcery in the name of Jesus of Nazareth.
9. I cancel I break it, and I cast out any unclean spirit of cancer that tries to establish itself in my lungs, my bones, my breasts, my throat, my back, my spine, my liver, my kidneys, in the pancreas, in my skin and my stomach in the name of Jesus of Nazareth.
10. I cancel, break, and cast out all unclean spirits that cause diabetes, high blood pressure, low blood pressure, heart attacks, strokes, kidney failure, leukemia, blood diseases, breathing problems, arthritis, lupus, and insomnia in the name of Jesus de Nazareth.
11. I cancel, and I cast out all hereditary curses of illness that cause discomfort and discouragement in the name of Jesus of Nazareth.

12. I cancel, break, and cast out all curses of premature death and destruction, in the name of Jesus of Nazareth
13. I declare and decree that I am free from any disease or illness because my Savior Jesus Christ took our sicknesses and infirmities upon Himself, so I now claim my position in Christ Jesus more than a winner.
14. I declare myself cured of .... (speak the name of the disease), in the name of the Lord Jesus Christ, I call perfect physical and organic health into my life
15. It is written that Jesus Christ carried our sins on His body, so we, dead to sins, may live for justice; by His wounds, we were healed. Amen.

PRAYER AGAINST SPIRIT OF INFIRMITIES

1. Heavenly father in the name of Jesus of Nazareth you said, in Isaiah 53: 4 surely, he bore our sicknesses and suffered our pains; and we considered him scourged, wounded by God, and dejected. But he was wounded for our rebellions, crushed for our sins; I declare by His stripes I was healed.
2. Heavenly father on behalf of Jesus of Nazareth, we take power and the authority of your written word; that whatever we bind on earth will be bound in heaven, and whatever we unleash on earth will be loosed in heaven.
3. In the name of JESUS OF NAZARETH, we activate that word, and we bind, We chain, we arrest, and we throw in the fire the spirit of CANCER, AIDS, LEUKEMIA, ALZHEIMER,

HUMAN PAPILLOMA, TUBERCULOSIS, HEPATITIS, PNEUMONIC PLAGUE, YELLOW FEVER, CHOLERA, OSTEOPOROSIS, LIVER DISEASE, ASTHMA, DENTAL CARIES, DIABETES, OBESITY, SYPHILIS, GENITAL LUPUS, HEART DISEASE, INFECTIONS, IMPOTENCE, HEMORRHOIDS, VARICES, CELLULITIS, DEAF, BLINDNESS, LEPROSY, PARALYSIS, GASTRITIS, CIRRHOSIS, EPILEPSY, COLITIS, HEMORRHOIDS, ARTHRITIS, INSANITY, CORONAVIRUS.

PRAYER AGAINST THE SPIRIT OF CANCER

Cancer has a name; therefore, it can be cured and controlled with a higher designation, which is the name of Jesus Christ. All we desire to look at is to apply a little faith and consistency in prayer until we get the expected results.

I experience how effective prayer can kill this spirit. This is a serious matter that concerns millions of people around the world. There are some instances where doctors have even given up hope, and all they hope for is for the person to take their last breathing. The suffering and agony of the cancer patient are incomprehensible; the recovery process is slower than its killing powers. However, there is marvelous news; God has promised that He will heal all our diseases if cancer is a disease so that God can heal it. Perhaps you are suffering from the disease; this could be the miracle you need to beat the disease.

1. I declare by the government of heaven that my healing is established in the name of Jesus.
2. I come against all the powers and principalities that want to hinder my healing process, and I destroy them by the power of resurrection.
3. I restore the suffering of cancer with consolation in the name of Jesus.
4. I destroy every lump in my chest in the name of Jesus.
5. Because Christ has paid for everything on the cross, the stripes on him are a pinch of evidence to show that he did. I sink into the power that raised Christ from the dead and decree that the resurrection's power of Jesus has healed me.
6. Lord, by the power of resurrection. You will arise at this time and do what only you can do in the name of Jesus.
7. Because it has been written that if any man speaks, that he speaks like an oracle from God, I decree that I am free from the shackles of breast cancer so that the pain of illness spreads in the name of Jesus.
8. Lord, you told prophet Ezekiel that you are the God of all flesh and that there is nothing impossible for you. If this is true, it means that my healing is NOW. I declare in the name of Jesus that you will rise and do what only you can do by the power of the resurrection.
9. Heavenly Father let the blood of Jesus comforts me during my moment of pain; I pray that the comforter does not leave my

side when I go through the burning torment of breast cancer in the name of Jesus.

10. Heavenly Father, your word says that we must ask, and it will be given to us. I ask you to make the pain disappear in the name of Jesus.

11. Lord God, I refuse to die from this disease; I decree that I am healed will in the name of Jesus.

12. Lord God, I ask you to give me the grace to endure until the hour of my miracle arrives. I decree that you will give me the strength to wait until you resolve this storm around me.

13. Father Lord, I pray for all the other breast cancer patients; I ask you to heal them miraculously. I pray that disease loses its power over our bodies by the power of the blood of Jesus.

PRAYER DESTRUCTION OF STRONGHOLDS

1. Heavenly Father, I declare that I live in the sanctuary of the Highest and rest in the shade of the Almighty. I can do everything in Him who strengthens me, who is Christ Jesus, who died and rose from the dead, who transferred me through His redemptive work from the old covenant to the new covenant made with the blood of Jesus.

2. At this moment, I declare that I am releasing my soul so that the Spirit of God can move freely and enter the deepest and deepest compartments of my soul, mind, emotions, and will.

3. Lord Jesus, by the power of Your blood, I declare that all the bonds, covenants, and agreements that I signed with rebellious angels, with fallen angels, and with demons, through sinful procedures, are undone.
4. I now declare that the old man was crucified with Christ so that it may destroy the body of sin, and those who are Christ's have crucified the flesh and now walk in the spirit.
5. Lord, it is written there is no condemnation for those who are in Christ Jesus. O Lord, they are undone by the blood of Jesus.
6. All the rights I gave to the spirits of darkness to dominate my mind through opinions, teachings, cultures, whether from genetics or the social lifestyle that I gained.
7. May all the mistakes and sophisms that have established themselves as false lords of my soul be canceled.
8. I now remove from the hands of Satan and his demons and fallen angels, all legal rights, in the name of Jesus Christ, that these spirits no longer have the right to continue deceiving me and wrongly using me.
9. I give power and authority to Christ Jesus over all my soul, mind, will and body.
10. I acknowledge that any diverting spirit, personality, human vessel, satanic device.
11. I release weapons of mass destruction upon their headquarters and wipe out all their risks and measures of punishment. I offer, take AND RULE their area by the authority of the Holy Ghost and in the name of our LORD Jesus.

12. I acknowledge that any diverting spirit, identity, human vessel, satanic device, or curse shall now cease operation in our finances, be permanently denied access, be blinded and deafened to any of our movements, and rendered mute. ALL missed opportunities, diverted, lost investments, stolen money, or goods shall be immediately returned hundred-fold.

13

PRAYER FOR FINANCES

Beloved Heavenly Father, I come to You in the name of the Lord Jesus Christ of Nazareth, the son of the living God, the Ones who defeated all hell and today made me a more than a victorious person in Christ Jesus.

1. Oh God of Abraham, Isaac, and Jacob, the Great "I Am" now I come in Your presence as a child dependent on Your grace and mercy. I open my heart so that the Holy Spirit will produce the fruits in my life of the spirit so I will receive the blessings of the cross of Calvary.

2. In the name of Jesus Christ, I strengthen myself in the Lord and the strength of His power and put on all the armor of God to defend myself and attack the empire of darkness.

3. And I will give you the hidden treasures, and the closely guarded secrets so that you know that I am Jehovah, the God of Israel, that I give you a name. Isaiah 45:03.

4. Lord God, in the name of the Lord Jesus Christ, I claim my position of material and spiritual prosperity that I have in the Lord Jesus Christ, for His sinless life, for His shed blood, for His death, for His resurrection and His glorification.

5. Thank God that Jesus already made himself miserable so I could be rich. Poverty and misery are under my feet.

6. Oh, Heavenly Father, I have been faithful in tithes and offerings, so now rebuke the devourer and open the floodgates of heaven and pour out blessings without measure on my life, in the name of Jesus.

7. Lord Jesus, by faith and in Your name, I break the chains and fetters of the curse of misery and poverty, I no longer accept this in my life and by the blood of Jesus I order these curses to be sent to the abyss and never to be rise against me.

8. I take possession by faith and the name of the Lord Jesus Christ of all the richness in Christ Jesus because I am a child of God, and I am more than a conqueror in Christ Jesus.

PRAYER FOR PROSPERITY

1. I believe the prophets and prosper in the name of Jesus of Nazareth. Everyone will call me blessed, and I will be a desirable land.
2. I give, and it will be given to me in good measure, pressed down, shaken, and overflowing.
3. I meditate on your word day and night so that whatever it may do, prosper. Open the windows of heaven over my life, and I will receive more than I can store.
4. Lord, teach me to take advantage and to go the way I must go. Jesus of Nazareth, you became poor so that through your poverty, I could be prospered.
5. There are goods and richness in my house because I fear you and take great delight in your commandments. My doors are continually open for the wealth of the nations to enter my bank accounts.
6. May my barns be filled with plenty, and my wine presses overflow with new wine. May my barns be full; May my cattle multiply to thousands in our fields.
7. May my houses be full of wheat, and my wine presses overflow with wine and oil. Prosper my lands and let me make the best of the fruits for your first fruits. Lead me to the valleys that flow in gold and diamonds in abundance.
8. I command divine order to be established in every dimension of our lives and the church's life.

9. May all grace abound in my house, and I lack nothing. Let my head be anointing with oil and let my barns be running over.
10. Let me see the abundance of heaps in my house. I love wisdom; I have my inheritance, and my treasures come in abundance.
11. Give me wealth and abundant business on this earth.
12. Support me with your grace, and your favor persecute me.
13. I am a child of God and take pleasure in my prosperity.

PRAYER FOR GETTING AND KEEPING A JOB

1. Lord Jesus, open a door of opportunity for me! Lord, answer this cry from the depths of my heart: open a door for me! Only You know, Jesus, the moment of difficulty for which I (say your name) and my entire family is going through unemployment.
2. You also know, Lord, with how much hope I approach You to ask you to go ahead of me, opening a door and preparing a job, so I can, through a job worthy, give my family the daily bread because you are my God, my hope. (Psalm 70-5)
3. I ask that you give me all the courage, confidence, fearlessness, and strength to leave my house in search of a job, in the certainty that Your hands, extended in my favor, will knock on that door before me, preparing to enter a career.
4. I thank you with all my heart because I believe that *"with God, nothing is impossible"* (Lk 1-37)

5. Heavenly Father, I seek protection under the wings of your hands; I come against all the enemy's plans to make me a victim of occupational danger in the name of Jesus. In the name of Jesus. I refuse to be the victim of any evil circumstance.
6. Father God, I pray that your right hand will guide me to your strength, and your spirit will ignite my inner man so he may work with the environment of your spirit and power by the power of the ascension.
7. Father God, I pray that your power and your glory will accompany me everywhere I go. Let your spirit help me put on all my spiritual armor to chase away every evil thing that wants to come my way today.
8. Father Lord, I ask that your power come before me and sanctify my workplace with Christ's precious blood.
9. By the power that raised Jesus from the dead, I destroy everything that has been programmed or planted by the enemy to cause me pain at work in the name of Jesus.
10. Lord, I entrust my life to your mighty hands when I left today.
11. I pray that your spirit will cast me aside and exempt me from whatever evil is planned to happen today.
12. I ask you to give your angels the burden on me that they will guide me in all my ways today.
13. By the power of the cross, I cover my desk with the blood of Jesus. No incriminating files will be shown in my office today.

14. I destroy the enemy scheme to get involved in my job. Lord throw confusion into the enemy's fields concerning me and because every tongue that revolts against me be destroyed by the power of the blood.
15. Lord Jesus, by my weapon of war, is not carnal but spiritual, I use your power and strength to attack the complete armor of God that will lead me away from evil in the name of Jesus.
16. I place my hope and trust you for victory over the enemy who wants to condemn me and kill me, and I cancel his plans in the name of Jesus.

PRAYER RELEASING FORGIVENESS

1. God, in the name of Jesus, in Your presence, I confess that I am bitter, disappointed, sad, and feeling under the hands of the executioners. I need to open the door of my heart so that You can enter and free me from all emotional discomfort when remembering scenes from the past. Although I lived under the yoke of death, under the influence of the executioners, I no longer accept the disturbance, torment, and deceit. Therefore, I reject Satan and his demons of anger, hatred, pride, withheld forgiveness, bitterness, and any accusation. I expel them from my soul and order them to leave and never return, in the name of Jesus
2. I ask the Holy Spirit to enable me to release and ask forgiveness from the people I have offended, according to His

direction, in a favorable time. I now take possession of the strength I need to proceed.

3. I choose and forgive all the people who have offended me (name the people) and wish them to be blessed with spiritual and material blessings in Christ Jesus.

4. Now, Lord, turn off ministering angels of divine healing to visit my soul, my heart, my conscience, and dislodge from my conscious and subconscious memory the trauma and emotional wounds. Minister Your Word, renewing me.

5. May Your Spirit work miraculously, make real spiritual surgeries in my life and sustain the decision of forgiveness that I make today. Operate, Lord, pouring out the fire that comes from the Throne of Grace to burn and destroy the chains, chains, and fetters, which prevent the understanding and action of forgiveness in my life.

6. May Your holy oil, the anointing of inner healing, be poured into me so that the flow of Your Spirit will heal wounds and traumas and set me free.

7. May the anointing of God fill me with Your grace and Your presence, drying and pulling out the roots of bitterness.

8. Lord, fill every void with the grace and richness in the glorious name of Jesus Christ, which meets all needs.

9. Lord, only You can do this work. The adjustments, the restoration in my heart, and I believe that I receive this healing starting today, in the name of Jesus. Amen.

PRAYER TO OBTAIN VISA /IMMIGRANT STATUS

We serve a God of all nations; no nation can resist a man or woman whom God has sent. If you need to be legal in a country or need a visa, you can use them. These prayer points are inspired, and before you begin to pray, you must first examine some factors.

Did God send you? Is it God's will to go to that country, or He wants you to live there legally? God will only support the envoys. If he didn't send you, you go or stay on your own, and you may not be successful. Therefore, you must pray for God's will first and make sure that it is God's will that you go to that country.

You must have a genuine reason and purpose to leave; there are many wrong reasons people want to leave a country and live in another. Regardless of your good intentions to travel abroad, you can still be denied a visa, that's where the prayers come in. These resident/visa prayer points will guide you as you pray all satanic obstacles out of your way. As you pray this prayer today, the God of heaven will grant you a supernatural favor in front of the consul or the immigration officer. Your visa interview will be successful, or you will; have your authorization to live. Pray these prayers today in faith and hope that God will do great work in your life in the name of Jesus.

1. Lord may all obstacles and barriers be removed on my journey, in the name of Jesus.
2. Lord, let every evil network designed against my success fall apart in the name of Jesus Christ.
3. Lord, let the spirit of favor and goodwill come into my life in the name of Jesus.
4. Lord, let each eye that monitors my journey's progress receive the arrows of fire by the power of our Lord Jesus Christ's blood and divine authority.
5. By the power of our Lord Jesus Christ's blood and divine authority, Lord Jesus Christ Let the angels of the living God roll the stone blocking the success of my visa, in the name of Jesus.
6. May God arise and may all the enemies that are secretly spoken against me be dispersed in the name of Jesus.
7. All the evil spirits, disguised to annoy me, are bound in the name of Jesus.
8. Oh Lord, make me find favor with the consul/immigration officer in the name of Jesus.
9. I deny the spirit of the tail and claim the head's spirit in my visa/residence approval in the name of Jesus.
10. I command that all negative responses planted by the devil in anyone's mind against my advancement be shattered in the name of Jesus.

11. Lord, transfer, remove, or change all human agents who are determined to prevent me from obtaining my visa/or residence in the name of Jesus.
12. Lord, help me identify and deal with any weaknesses in me that may hinder my progress.
13. I bind each delegated strongman to hinder my progress in the name of Jesus.
14. I command to put to flight all the enemies of my advances, in the name of Jesus.
15. I bind and renounce your spirit of awful luck related to the approval of my visa in the name of Jesus.
16. I reject the word "no" and another negative answer during my visa /immigration interview in the name of Jesus.

PRAYER OF RENEWING THE MIND

1. Lord Jesus, I invoke Your name so You may judge and curse the demons that make me think thoughts contrary to Your will. I tie these demons, in the name of Jesus, so that I can think only of Your Word, Lord.
2. Lord Jesus, I choose and decide to think only Your thoughts; I reject and renounce the thoughts of Satan and his followers.
3. I recognize that only Your Word is a powerful weapon to destroy the strongholds of my mind. Your word is a powerful weapon to destroy all the advice and all the pride that rises to prevent me from knowing God. Your name is mighty for me

to take all thought and my mind bound to obey Christ. Your word is powerful to avenge, judge, and curse all disobedience. I regret thinking about Satan's opinions and not Your thoughts, Lord.

4. Lord Jesus, make me, from today, think only of what is real and just. Everything pure and lovely; whatever is of good fame, whatever occupies my mind.

5. Lord may my thoughts be full of mercy and good fruit, without partiality and hypocrisy. All this I want to think about so that the name of God is exalted and glorified. Amen.

6. Great God, in the name of the Lord Jesus, I understand that I am here now, exposing myself totally to You, in spirit, soul, and body so that You will be carried out in my being. Here I am, Lord, I authorize the Holy Spirit, who is the Ones who corrects, disciplines, and applies the cross that is Your Word, to bring renewal in my mind.

7. I know that my mind is an enemy of God because I see my sin, my transgression every day. Therefore, Lord, I cannot change it, but one thing I can before You, I decide, I open the door of my heart and say that You can act and fight against the demons that make up the ego, the old life that still exists in my heart.

8. Lord, take off, dethrone, and turn off the powers of darkness in my life, remove the influence of demons, the evil empire that makes me have mistakes and illusions about myself and my Creator, my Lord, and the Holy Spirit.

9. Lord Jesus, from now on, I ask You that the anointing of Your Spirit, enter my soul as Joshua entered the land of Canaan to defeat the demons, the spirits of darkness, displacing and emptying all the territories of my conscious and subconscious, of my will and my emotions. You have the authority to enter with the Sword of the Spirit, with the fire of the throne, with the blood of the Lamb, to change and transform the story of my life.

10. Lord, I want to be a vessel and keep the commandment, God's command of the vocation to which I was called to be a member of the body of Your Son Jesus Christ.

11. Use me from now on, Lord, in the function and position that You placed me in the Body of Christ. Make me subject to the spirit, to the Christ, who is my head. All deceptions come out now, be dispelled by the light that is the Word of God. I want to be trained and not just informed.

12. As of today, I release all the work of the spirit to apply the cross of Christ on the old nature; I want to be resurrected with Christ Jesus. Amen!

PRAYER AGAINST THE ATTACKS OF THE CHURCH

Some attacks are launched against the Church. Often these attacks come from the government of darkness to take up arms against the Church. Meanwhile, any battle against the Church is a war against Jesus Christ. Interestingly, the devil hates the gathering of brothers because when believers unite in agreement to prayer, God will hear the prayer and deliver an answer. That is why the first thing the devil intends to attack is the peace of the Church. Another thing important to know is that the Church is not the physical building or the structure, but that the people are the Church.

Knowing that attacks are being launched against the Church, it is pertinent that we pray to God to free the Church and rescue from the hands of the destroyer. The devil uses human beings to attack the Church many times, and men are its driving force against the Church. Therefore, religion and church leaders must always strive to pray that the Church is not a victim of the devil's attack on the Church. When an attack is launched against the Church, it is not for us to flee as believers.

1. Heavenly Father says that the enemies will surely come together, but in the name of Jesus, they will not succeed.
2. Lord, we oppose every attack that the enemy is organizing for the Church and void them by the power in the name of Jesus.
3. I decree the fire of God on any meeting that does not want the Church to succeed in its purpose on earth; I destroy them with the fire of the Holy Ghost.
4. Heavenly Father, your purpose for the Church will not be satisfied if the battle hits the Church. We destroy every arrow that is thrown at the Church, and we kill it in the name of Jesus.

5. We come against every evil and demonic gathering against the Church, and we pray that the fire of the Almighty God will consume the enemy in the name of Jesus.
6. Father, we ask that regarding the Church, your council and council only remain. Let the Lamb's blood destroy all the enemy's schedules that plan to delay the plan of God.
7. We destroy all attacks of evil in our lives in the name of Jesus.
8. Father, we ask for spiritual strength to identify the enemy's tricks that could cause the Church to miss her purpose in the name of Jesus.
9. The purpose of your Church is to free people from spiritual darkness; any power or scheme that wants to hinder the Church must be blinded in the name of Jesus.
10. Heavenly Father, I come before you this day because of the relentless attacks of the false demonic holy prophets who will not let rest. I announce victory over them in the name of Jesus.
11. Lord God, I ask you to rise in your anger and do justice to every group of people who deceive people with your name. I pray that you rise and destroy each group of people who pretended to be in your name.
12. Lord, the scripture says that no armed weapon against me will prosper. I come against every attack by the evil Church on my life and that of my family in the name of Jesus.
13. Lord God, I pray for the spiritual power and meaning that will triumph over all your attacks in the name of Jesus.

14. I decree the fire of Almighty God on each group of people who intend to harm me or cause me pain, let the inextinguishable fire of the throne of God consume them right now in the name of Jesus.

PRAYER AGAINST RELIGIOUS SPIRITS

1. Great and Eternal God, I glorify Your name Father and ask forgiveness for my mistakes and sins.
2. Lord, I acknowledge that I have broken Your law; I have lived in rebellion to Your commandment. Forgive me for not understanding Your will and forgive me for not understanding what the Church is. I ask You, Lord, remove evil, religious spirits, and place the love of Christ in my heart.
3. In the name of Jesus, I remove legalism and dogmas, remove religious customs, remove religion and tradition from my heart, which prevents me from walking according to Your will.
4. I give freedom for Your Spirit to act in my life and enable me to read, study, and obey Your Word so that Your prosperity will come over my life. Oh Lord, I praise You and thank You in the name of the Lord Jesus.

PRAYER AGAINST JEALOUSY AND ANXIETY

- In the name of Jesus, Lord remove the envy, jealousy, selfishness, hatred, anxiety, and greed from my heart.

- Oh Lord, take the bitterness and depression out of me. Give me your spirit's conviction that I need to change and that I need to depend on Your Spirit.
- Oh Lord, unmask the deception of Satan in my soul with Your powerful Light. I ask You, Lord, remove the spirit of unbelief and spiritual blindness from my mind. Lord, burn the strongholds that harden my heart. Amen.

PRAYER AGAINST CURSES AND LUST OF THE FLESH

1. Beloved God, in the name of the Lord Jesus Christ, and by faith, I come before You this day, and I am convinced that You love me. You sent Your Son to break this curse of the lust of the flesh and greed. I now order gluttony to cease the operation in my life at this very moment. I will never again have this problem in the name of Jesus. I give this gluttony to the Lord Jesus Christ, for He has already set me free. He took the test for me and passed 100% points. So, I have the points He won on the test. I have the power of His name and, therefore, by that name, a name that protects me and by His Blood that purifies me immediately, I am released by the blood of the Lord Jesus Christ.

2. Now, Satan, you and your excessive demons, the addiction to eating, the lust of the flesh, have heard the prayer I just said, your strength and your dominion over my life have now been broken in my life, in the name of Jesus. I will never again be a

slave to greed. I am free because the Lord Jesus Christ has set me free. I am more than a winner in Christ Jesus. Now, Lord, I ask that you enable me to lose weight and that in the name of Jesus, I maintain my ideal weight. I thank you and praise you, Lord Jesus.

PRAYER FOR SANCTIFICATION

1. Eternal God, in the name of your Son Jesus Christ, I arrive in your presence at this moment. I want to exalt and glorify the name of the Lord, my Savior, your only son, who became the firstborn among many that you will raise. At this moment, I know that there is no good in me, and now Lord, I authorize the power of God in the Holy Spirit that dwells in me to be free to fight all the evil forces that occupy and dominate the functions of my soul. I now reject and renounce all the evil spirits that have influence and dominion over my mind, my will, and my emotions.

2. I authorize the Holy Spirit to fight and dethrone and remove these beings' domination from my soul.

3. I fully authorize the Holy Spirit's action to win because I know that I can do nothing by myself without Christ. At this moment, I authorize the Spirit of the living Christ to enter my soul and cleanse it with the Lamb's blood.

4. Lord Jesus, I open my heart so that now you might strengthen my inner man powerfully with the heavenly richness that Christ has given me.

5. By grace in Christ Jesus, I release the action of the Spirit of Christ so that He will take root in my heart and, from there, command all things in my soul.

6. Lord, use this vessel to build Your economic plan. I give freedom so that the Spirit of Christ makes me empty of idols and makes me useful for the divine economy because I was called to be a member of the Body of Christ. So, devil, you are no longer allowed to use me against my God, because I no longer belong to you. Look at my life and see that I am a new creature in Christ Jesus. Look at the pure blood that shed on the cross of Calvary and see how victorious I am already, even though I am still living in the soul, in obstinacy. In slavery to demons, I am already victorious through Christ Jesus. Amen.

PRAYER TO BREAK OF ALLIANCES AND CURSES

1. Beloved Heavenly Father, in the name of the Lord Jesus Christ and through the blood of Jesus, I declare all covenants, all agreements, all contracts, and all ties that my ancestors and I have made with hell and demons or unconsciously. At this moment, I release forgiveness for my ancestors and me, too, because we were the agents that caused these hereditary curses to reach me.

2. Lord Jesus Christ, I now confess my sins and those of my ancestors, from the first to the fourth generation, because they have prevaricated against You, and I have also done what was not pleasant before You. Therefore, by Your mercy, I receive Your forgiveness for the precious blood of Jesus.
3. Heavenly Father, for Christ's atoning sacrifice and His resurrection that made me a new creature, and Your Word tells us that there is no condemnation for those who are in Christ Jesus. Therefore, I am already free because Christ has set me free.
4. I declare all curses disconnected from my life, and I link in my life all the blessings arising from the cross of Calvary. Thank you, Jesus, thank you, my Heavenly Father. Amen

PRAYER TO DESTROY EVIL LOCKS

When a devilish agent hits a padlock with evil force, he calls the victim's name, utters curses and dirty words, before closing the lock and keeping or hiding the keys. Sometimes evil agents throw the key to their evil locks into the water of the river. Sometimes evil agents throw the key to their evil padlock in the forest or bury it. There are even padlocks, shaped only and expressly for these evil practices. These padlocks have no keys and are used by evil guys to perform these merciless operations. The majority of witchcraft agents use evil padlocks: satanic priests, false prophets, and impious and violent men.

PRAYER POINTS

1. All my potential locked up in the convents of darkness, I unlock you now with the power of the blood, in the name of Jesus (declare it x 7 times).
2. My destiny, I unlock you now, get out of the prison of witchcraft in the name of Jesus.
3. Any chain of sorcery that encloses the potentials of my family break yourself by fire in the name of Jesus (declare it x 7 times).
4. I free my life and my family from the bondage of ancestral idols in the name of Jesus.
5. I release my breakthroughs from the dark convent in the name of Jesus (declare it x 7 times).
6. My possessions locked in the evil altars! Be free by the Blood of Jesus in the name of Jesus.
7. You, evil altar which encloses my resources, receive the fire of God and burn in ashes in the name of Jesus.
8. I unlock all the evil padlocks, and I release all my resources, my potential, my breakthroughs locked up in the name of Jesus (declare it x 7 times).
9. Any foundation of witchcraft in my family I lock you in the celestial padlock in the name of Jesus.
10. Evil enemy padlocks used against my family and me, I command you, in the mighty name of Jesus, lock up your owners.
11. Enemies of my foundation, I lock up your powers and I chain you with iron and fire bolts in the name of Jesus.

12. Any enemy of my enlargement, I lock you in the celestial padlock in the name of Jesus (declare it x 7 times).
13. Any assembly of witchcraft, in the sky, in the air, on the earth, in the forest, I padlock the air against you in the name of Jesus.
14. All power that supports and strengthens the enemies of my breakthroughs, I padlock you with the iron and fire bolts in the name of Jesus.
15. I break the spine of every spirit that speaks against me and I destroy its root by the blood of Jesus.
16. I unlock all the evil padlocks, and I release all my resources, my potential, my breakthroughs locked up in the name of Jesus (declare it x 7 times).

14

PRAYER FOR MARRIAGE THAT IS GOING THROUGH PROBLEMS

If marriage is a divine covenant, why is it so difficult to prevent the sanctity of love from being contaminated by suspicion? If we commit to each other at the Lord's altar, if we promise to love one another, in joy, in health and sickness, every day of our lives, how suddenly has our relationship turned into fights and indifference?

From one of my spiritual daughters: "My marriage is going through a great conflict that seems endless, and when I think this phase is over, it starts all over again. There are days when our conversations are like pins, like thorns in the flesh: everything looks like accusation and offense. Everything becomes suspicious, everything we say turns into verbal aggression; everything is a reason to return to past facts and errors, and we only see each other's defects. Sometimes I wonder if my marriage will survive the challenges I am experiencing." Today, I discovered that the perfect marriage does not exist, and I want to learn to deal with imperfections from now on. I want to live every moment of my marriage, knowing that the relationship always needs a stimulus and an effort to see the other's qualities more than its defects. We got married to support each other and together to overcome the difficulties we could not face alone.

The response I provided to the spiritual daughter helped the family to be restored: "you need to teach and to trust each other and trust God in the toughest moments, and to love, in moments of disagreement; to be silent in the face of verbal and critical offenses; to believe; to resign yourself to an accusing look; to understand the other in the face of threats, of abandonment, of separation; fighting for marriage when the other says there is no more love because in God, love never ends. May God give you the courage and serenity to face situations and wisdom to seek solutions May God show you how to forgive, and may all resentment be washed from your soul by His redeeming blood".

PRAYER TO CANCEL DIVORCE

1. Beloved Heavenly Father, I thank you for the perfect plan that you devised for our marriage. I know that a marriage that

works in your will and receives your blessings is satisfying and pleasant. By divine authority, I place our marriage before you so you can make it exactly what You want it to be. Please forgive my sins of failure in our marriage.

2. By the power of the blood, I overthrow Satan's strongholds, who intend to destroy our marriage.
3. I interrupt all relationships between us by Satan and his evil spirits, in the name of the Lord Jesus Christ.
4. I will only accept the relationships established by You and the divine Holy Spirit. I ask the Holy Spirit to enable me to relate to _____ (quote the name of the spouse) in a way that meets your needs.
5. I submit to you our physical relationship so he can enjoy your blessings.
6. I submit our love to you so you can grow and increase. I want to know and experience in marriage the fullness of your perfect will.
7. Lord, open the eyes of _____ (quote the name of the spouse) so he/she can perceive all the lies of Satan directed against him/her.
8. I order that all curses that have been issued against my marriage will be canceled and returned by the power of the blood.
9. Through the Blood of Jesus, I wash off all demonic marks of marital unrest in the name of Jesus

10. Every spirit inherited from my father's or mother's house fighting against my marriage is gone forever, in the name of Jesus.
11. Let the effect of each ceremony performed on my wedding day, and which has been working against me, be canceled and destroyed, in the name of Jesus.
12. Any negative information whispered against my marriage, or married life is crushed in the name of Jesus.
13. Each spiritual dowry collected in my name, I return to the sender, in the name of Jesus.
14. Any power that says I will not enjoy my married life will be destroyed now! In the name of Jesus.
15. I order my husband/wife to escape, to return, in the name of Jesus.
16. Your spirit of matrimonial destruction was tied in the name of Jesus.
17. I command that every curse in my marriage be turned into a blessing in the name of Jesus.
18. I order that every evil that strange friends have made against my home be reversed, in the name of Jesus.

PRAYER INTERCESSION FOR CHILDREN

1. I humbly kneel before my heavenly Father to intercede for my child_____(quote your child's name). I place him/her before You, in the name of the Lord Jesus Christ.

2. I put all the work of the Lord Jesus Christ in focus directly against the powers of darkness that blinded and bound the_____(say your child's name).
3. I proclaim the victory of the incarnation, the crucifixion, the resurrection, the ascension and the glorification of our Lord Jesus Christ directly against all the power of Satan in the life of _____ (say the name of your child). I bind all the powers of the unleashed darkness to destroy the_____ (say the name of your child), and I free you from your blindness in the name of our Lord Jesus Christ.
4. I invite the Holy Spirit to work in the heart of_____ (quote your child's name), to convince him of sin, justice, and future judgment.
5. I confess the sins of _____ (quote your child's name) in front of You, and I beg Your compassionate mercy towards Him/her. I confess his/her subjection to every kind of sin of the flesh that he/she has given Satan a place in his/her life.
6. I pray that Christ's blood will cover my daughter's /son's evil and hope in the Holy Spirit to lead him/her to repentance, faith and life in the Lord Jesus Christ.
7. By faith, I call you to a life of submission and service to the living and true God, in the name of the Lord Jesus Christ. Amen.
8. May God give you a spirit of excellence and be responsible for all your relationships. (Daniel 6: 3)

9. Let them submit entirely to God and resist the devil. (James 4: 7)
10. May the Holy Spirit pour out wisdom and grace on parents to sow eternal values in their children's hearts.
11. May the Spirit of Life cleanse the air of all evil that spreads through the mass media to steal the purity, innocence and sanctity of children.

15

PRAYER OF OVERCOMING THE FLESH

Lord Jesus, I ask you to take control of my heart and use it only for your glory. I decree that the lust of the flesh will not ruin my life in the name of Jesus.

1. I decree the lust of the flesh will not destroy my destiny. I declare by the divine authority my marriage is secured in the name of Jesus.
2. I come against all the devil's plans to destroy my marriage; I destroy his plans by the blood of Jesus. From now on, I refuse to be a slave to sexual immoralities in the name of Jesus.

3. Lord guide me and take me in your hands so I will not be a victim of evil temptations in the name of Jesus.
4. I refuse to fall into sin again; I refuse to remain a slave to the enemy's deductions. From now on, I am a free man because I belong to Jesus.
5. Beloved Heavenly Father, it is by faith that I appropriate death today with the Lord Jesus Christ on the cross. I appropriate all the benefits of the crucifixion through my union with Christ on the cross.
6. I consider myself dead to my old nature, to the flesh, and all the works of the flesh through my union with Christ on the cross.
7. I recognize that my old nature always tries to be resurrected to rise against the Lord and His will for my life, but I want to leave the dead flesh with my Lord Jesus on the cross. I am grateful that this absolute truth can be my subjective experience.
8. I recognize that the appropriation of the death of my flesh is an essential step towards victory over these temptations of the flesh that slap me because it is written that flesh called flesh and spirit called spirit.
9. I was born of water and the spirit; I am a new creature, and I will no longer be guided by the flesh, in the name of Jesus I will be conducted only by the Holy Spirit of God because it is also written that the one who joins the Lord is a Spirit with Him.

PRAYER AGAINST THE ADVERSARIES

1. Beloved Heavenly Father, I praise You because Satan is defeated. I am glad that the Lord Jesus Christ ministered this defeat in His sinless life. I look forward to the day when the Lord Jesus Christ will reign, and Satan will be bound in the abyss.

2. I know that Satan will finally be thrown into the lake of fire, prepared for him and his angels forever. I am glad that today, in my union with Christ, you give me total victory over Satan.

3. I take my victory with determination and claim my position as more than a winner for the Ones who loved me, Jesus Christ. I refuse to be continually defeated by Satan in any area of my life. He cannot dominate me and will not do it, for I am dead with Christ for his domain.

4. I say that God's grace and mercy dominate all areas of my life through union with Christ. Grant me the grace, Lord, to affirm Your victory even when life's experiences seem to contradict it.

5. Thank you for those battles and everything in your wisdom and design you are trying to accomplish.

6. I accept the battle, and I rejoice in Your purpose. I gladly accept and wish to enjoy all Your goal in allowing Satan's kingdom to come to me.

7. I reject all of Satan's attempts. Through the victory of my Savior Jesus Christ, I remain resolutely and firmly in the

certainty of my success. Confident, I wait on you, Lord Jesus Christ of Nazareth.

8. When Your purpose for that battle is fulfilled, I know that it will be lost in the obscurity of forgotten battles and the defeated enemy. So, it will be for the name of the Lord Jesus Christ. Amen!

PRAYER TO DISCREDIT THE ENEMY

1. Let the enemy be ashamed and troubled, turn, and be ashamed suddenly (Psalms 6:10). Make me a sign for good and to be seen by those who hate me and be ashamed (Psalms 86:17). Shame and confuse those who seek my life (Psalms 35: 4).

2. Let those who rejoice in my evil dress in shame (Psalms 35:26). Spread your bones and shame them (Psalm 53: 5).

3. Let those who follow my existence be embarrassed and confounded, let those who desire my evil be turned back and ashamed (Psalms 70: 2). Fill their faces with shame (Psalm 83:16).

4. May all who are hot with you be ashamed (Isaiah 45:24). May those who revolt against me be ashamed (Psalm 109: 28). May the proud spirits be ashamed (Psalm 119: 78).

PRAYER AGAINST CONDEMNATION

1. Lord of Hosts, in the Name of Your Son Jesus Christ of Nazareth, I want at this moment to praise You, to thank You for the forgiveness, for the sonship and for the eternal life that I gained through the Cross of Calvary. This sacrifice was perfect and effective because today I am united with Christ Jesus above all principalities, all powers, and all dominators.

2. I declare that there is no condemnation for those who are in Christ Jesus. Look at my life, Satan, and contemplate the Light of Christ, the Blood of the Lamb that is on my life, guaranteeing my salvation.

3. At this moment, in the authority of the Name and Blood of Jesus, I declare myself disconnected from all curses, both in the natural world and in the spiritual dimension, the whole covenant, all the pact, all the bond, all the agreement and all the bonds, the entire contract, from my ancestors who may have prevaricated against my God and His Word.

4. I confess to you all these sins, and I forgive all of them and declare myself disconnected from these hereditary curses by the Blood of Jesus.

5. I declare, oh Father, in the Name of Jesus Christ that all condemnations or curses from my contemporary life be disconnected, in all areas, whether in acting, speaking, or thinking. By Your mercy, O Father, and by the Blood of Jesus, I receive Your forgiveness and declare myself free from all curses.

6. I now bind myself in the Lord and the strength of His power and declare that my ego, the life of my soul, is wholly subjugated to the dominion of the Holy Spirit. Amen.

PRAYER TO PASS AN EXAM

These prayers for success at any exam you are preparing to take in the name of Jesus. The Holy Spirit will empower your study life and give you direction as you read and a caring mind to help you excel in your official exam in the name of Jesus. Pray these prayers with faith today and receive your success in the name of Jesus. Congratulations.

1. You spirit of Watching, I paralyze you and order you to be roasted in the name of Jesus.
2. I break the evil cycle of failure in my exam (Mention the name of the exam or Subject), in the name of Jesus.
3. You strong man sitting in my success, do not be carried away by the thunder of God, in the name of Jesus.
4. Blood of Jesus, protect my existence against every spell
5. I turn down the spirit of inattention; I dismiss the spirit of distraction, and I deny the spirit of wrongdoing in the name of Jesus.
6. Let every movement of obscurity in my academics fail sadly, in the name of Jesus.

7. I am against all spirit of failure, in the name of Jesus.
8. I reject all the evil manipulations of my destiny in the name of Jesus.
9. I receive retentive memory, boldness, and a healthy mind, in the name of Jesus.
10. I release myself from all spirit of confusion and error in the name of Jesus.
11. Father Lord put your hand of fire on my memory and give me retentive memory, in the name of Jesus.
12. Lord, keep me diligent in my special preparations.
13. Lord, I dedicated all my faculties to you, in the name of Jesus.
14. That all the evil mechanisms destined to change my destiny are frustrated in the name of Jesus.

WARFARE PRAYER FOR ALL OCCASIONS

1. May all unprofitable stations of my goodness be silenced in the name of Jesus.
2. May all blessings confiscated by the spirits of witchcraft be released in the name of Jesus.
3. May all blessings confiscated by familiar spirits be released in the name of Jesus.
4. May all blessings confiscated by ancestral spirits be released in the name of Jesus.
5. May all blessings confiscated by envious enemies be released in the name of Jesus.

6. I bind every prince of darkness who speaks against me in the name of Jesus of Nazareth.
7. I bind the kings with shackles and the nobles with iron chains in the name of Jesus of Nazareth.
8. I bind every spirit of love for money that leads to destruction in the name of Jesus of Nazareth.
9. I bind every prince of darkness who persecutes me and sexually harasses me in the name of Jesus.
10. I bind and rebuke any impure bird that wants to nest in my head in the name of Jesus of Nazareth.
11. I bind and rebuke any spirit that wants to slip away at night in my life in the name of Jesus of Nazareth.
12. I veto and send into the lagoon of fire mental control of the octopus and squid, in the name of Jesus of Nazareth.
13. I bind every sea monster that wants to attack my life or my business in the name of Jesus of Nazareth.
14. I bind Leviathan and every proud spirit that comes against my life in the power of your word.
15. I veto and send into the lagoon of fire Beelzebub, the lord of flies, in the name of Jesus of Nazareth.
16. I bind and destroy all swarms of flies that want to hinder my communion with the Holy Spirit.
17. I bind all spirits of hatred and corruption and racism towards my country in the name of Jesus of Nazareth.
18. I rebuke the terrors of death and destruction in the name of Jesus of Nazareth.

19. I bind fear and panic that comes through terrorism in the name of Jesus of Nazareth.
20. I bind every unclean spirit I incubate succubus who wants to attack me at night in the name of Jesus of Nazareth.
21. I bind and destroy every nightmare and demonic dream at night, in the name of Jesus of Nazareth.
22. I bind and rebuke any python who wants to restrict my prayer life, in the name of Jesus of Nazareth.
23. I confine and deactivate all activities of the devil in the name of Jesus.
24. I bind and rebuke any unclean spirit who works through the pelican in the name of Jesus of Nazareth.
25. I bind the night monster that works through the owl in the name of Jesus of Nazareth.
26. I bind every sea monster that wants to attack my life or my business in the name of Jesus of Nazareth.
27. I bind and rebuke any Goliath spirit who wants to challenge me in the valley in the name of Jesus of Nazareth.
28. I bind and rebuke all the deities and demons that work through the sun, in the name of Jesus of Nazareth.
29. I bind and rebuke all black, red, and yellow horses that operate against me in the name of Jesus of Nazareth.
30. I bind and throw into the lake of fire all the flies that want to affect my anointing, in the name of Jesus of Nazareth.
31. I bind and destroy the poison of every cobra that wants to spit its garbage in my mind in the name of Jesus of Nazareth.

32. I bind and destroy every red eagle of terror that comes against my nation and my family in the name of Jesus of Nazareth.
33. I bind and rebuke any religious terrorist who wants to destroy humanity in the name of Jesus of Nazareth.
34. I bind I rebuke any terrorist who conspires against my life and my nation in the name of Jesus of Nazareth.
35. I bind and rebuke any serpent who wants to get entangled or coiled in my life in the name of Jesus of Nazareth.
36. I bind and rebuke every vampire spirit who works against my finances at night in the name of Jesus of Nazareth.
37. I bind and rebuke every eagle, and demonic hawk sent against me to harm me in the name of Jesus of Nazareth.
38. I deny and cast into the lake of fire any demon that operates in my family and could enter my mind and heart in the name of Jesus of Nazareth.
39. I bind and throw into the lake of fire every thieving spirit who wants to steal my finances, my clients, my businesses, and my assets in the name of Jesus of Nazareth.
40. I bind and cast out every unclean spirit that tries to keep me in poverty, misery, scarcity, and financial deprivation in the name of Jesus of Nazareth.
41. I bind Satan and all his demons of deception who want to deviate me from the truth in any way in the name of Jesus of Nazareth into the lake of fire.

42. I bind and throw into the lake of fire every spirit of sorcery, witchcraft, magic, and fortune-telling who wants to deceive me in the name of Jesus of Nazareth.

43. I bind and cast out every desert spirit, the desert fox, and the dragon in the name of Jesus of Nazareth.

44. I bind and rebuke any unclean spirit of hatred, murder, and destruction who wants to manifest itself through terrorism in the name of Jesus of Nazareth.

45. I bind and throw into the lake of fire all the devil's anger directed at my life, my family, my children, my property, my business and finances in the name of Jesus of Nazareth.

CONCLUSION

The critical thing to remember in our war against Satan is this: SATAN IS DEFEATED! We do not have to defeat Satan; Christ has already overcome him on Calvary. Although Satan is defeated, he has not yet been cast into the lake of fire. He is free and working as hard as ever to keep unsaved in his Kingdom as God's servants, you and I must proclaim the gospel to the unsaved and deliver them from the power of Satan. The Lord Jesus revealed that if you wish to draw valuables out of a strong man's house, you must first tie the strong man. Satan is the "strong man", and his "assets" are the people he keeps under his power. If we are to deliver people from the power of Satan, we must first bind his power.

God has given you a powerful weapon to use against Satan, but it is useless if you don't use it. So, take Calvary's victory. Suppose Satan attacks your home. There are harsh words and bitter feelings. What should you do? Claim the victory of Calvary and bind the strong man, which is Satan. The apostle, Paul said: We have no fight against blood and flesh, but against principalities, against powers, against the rulers of the darkness of this century, against spiritual hosts of wickedness in the heavenly regions (Ephesians 6:12). When we perceive the times, we are now living that we are at war with Satan, the remnants will rise to pray for all things and without ceasing.

End-times intercessors understand that they must pray against problems in the home and in church. Pray for believers. Pray for the unconverted friends and family. The announcers of the gospel need prayer to advance God's kingdom. Pray fervently.

Don't give up!

The vital thing to be successful in prayer is perseverance. This means DO NOT GIVE UP. Keep praying until the answer comes to you. It requires time for God to deal with human wills. It takes time to change situations. God wants us to persevere in prayer, making Calvary's victory our own. The Lord Jesus said: "It is necessary to pray always, and not to faint."

Talking about spiritual warfare is essential to create awareness of the invisible world in the lives of believers. This mental fight is the one that the Christian and the church carry out together with the angelic hosts against the spiritual powers of evil.

The Bible frequently describes the Christian life as continuous spiritual warfare. The participation of Christians is not optional but obligatory from the invisible world's framework that eventually ends up moving to the natural.

While we are preparing for Jesus's return, the members of the Churches cannot be neutral towards the enemy, since that way we would disobey the word of the Lord who asks us to be attentive to the attacks of the enemy. In his word, God clarifies that we are in a constant spiritual battle against the principalities and powers of evil, which try to destroy the church and frustrate its task of world evangelization. Satan's goal is to destroy the church so that the gospel stops being preached.

We know our needs to take on the whole armor of God and engage in this wrestling with the divine weapons of integrity and prayer, as we perceive the action of our adversary, not merely in distorted philosophies outside the church but also within it, in the false gospels that distort the Scriptures and put the man in place of God. We need vigilance and discernment to safeguard the biblical gospel. We must consider the possibility that the Blessing Houses can organize themselves and have special days of prayer, fasting, vigils, and everything the Holy Spirit wants to do through those who attend them this March. The concept of spiritual warfare is spreading rapidly among evangelical churches, but now is the right time for each church to rise to practice what they have learned in these years. The Kingdom is in constant conflict with the power of darkness; the struggle occurs in the heavenly regions and is expressed in everything created on a personal, collective, and structural level. If we battle together, we will have significant victories.

Aggressive "war prayer" against these territorial spirits will lead citizens to repentance for their sins and immediate surrender to the Lord Jesus. If we pray continually, we will break the powers of the spiritual authorities that hold people. For this purpose, it is fundamental that the churches have an active intercessory leadership and that they are understood in Spiritual warfare.

We should also consider that the times we use for intercession must be led by committed leaders who lead the prayer teams to intercede under revelation so that the territorial spirits fall through prayer. In this prayer guide, there must be reasons directed by specific neighborhoods, powers, principalities that dominate them. One must intercede for governments, hospitals, police, but spiritual warfare must always reveal to disrupt the spirits that operate in those places. We pray for ourselves and others because we know that it is God who has the privilege. Prayer is our technique of communication with God. It is how we access His power and participate in His plans for this world. In prayer, we praise God and seek His face so we can be more like Him. We pray that God will soften people's hearts and lead them to salvation. We pray that He will encourage and grow His children. Ultimately, we pray that God's will be done in our lives and the lives of others.

The warfare prayer end times is the direct attack on territorial spirits who want to dominate forever the city where we live. When we begin to pray under the cloak of spiritual warfare, it is when these spirits release everything they had tied.

ABOUT THE AUTHOR

Pastor Elou Fleurine is the Senior Pastor of King Jesus Haitian Ministry in Homestead, Florida, under the covering of his spiritual father, Apostle Guillermo Maldonado. Pastor Elou and his wife, Widza are dedicated to building God's Kingdom one family at a time. His life is dedicated to living by example and encouraging men and women to live up to their full potential in Christ.

Pastor Elou has more than a decade of teaching and counseling family, enabling him to reach others with humor, warmth, transparency, and strength. He is a father, author, teacher, conference speaker, role model, and mentor. He is called to coach the believers in the area of deliverance, healing, and spiritual warfare.

Pastor Elou believes in the supernatural. He ministers the word of God with a prophetic insight and apostolic grace. Pastor Elou is a theologian holding both Bachelor's degree and Master's in Business Administration. He also holds a Bachelor's degree in Law. He is a former congressman of Haiti. He resides in Miami, Florida, with his wife Widza partner in ministry.

ACKNOWLEDGMENTS

Many people have helped me in bringing this book into shape. I would like to thank for their help throughout my life, without whom I would not be who I am or doing what I do. I would like to acknowledge and thank those who have had the most significant impact on this book's success.

All praise, honor, and glory to my Lord Jesus Christ for His most precious grace and mercy for this book's accomplishment. I could never have done this without the faith I have in you, the Almighty God.

Thank you to my mother, Lizanie Fleurine, for guiding me as a person. Words cannot express how grateful I am to you for all the sacrifices you have made on my behalf.

Thank you, Widza, my wonderful wife and best friend. You inspire me every day with your incredible thoughtfulness, love for prayer, and devotion to being as Christ-like as possible. Your prayer for me was what sustained me thus far.

I would like to thank my spiritual father and mother, Apostle Guillermo, and Ana Maldonado for the opportunity to receive the resources for being a part of this tremendous Apostolic ministry of King Jesus Ministry that opens my eyes to understand the supernatural.

Finally, my deepest gratitude to my dearest spiritual children at King Jesus Haitian Ministry in Homestead for their constant prayers and support. Thank you for your prayer.

www.ingramcontent.com/pod-product-compliance
Lightning Source LLC
Chambersburg PA
CBHW032123090426
42743CB00007B/448